USBORNE
IMPROVE YOUR ENGLISH

Rachel Bladon, Nicole Irving & Victoria Parker

Designed by Isaac Quaye, Diane Thistlethwaite & Michael W. Wheatley

Illustrated by Kevin Faerber & Colin Mier

Educational consultants:
Jane Davage, Phillipa Ferst, Angie Graham,
Valerie Munro and George Phillipson

Edited by Jane Chisholm

With thanks to Corinne Stockley and Rachael Swann

CONTENTS

SPELLING

CONTENTS

Niether or *neither*? *Pursue* or *persue*? After using this book you will have no doubt which are the correct spellings. Don't despair if you think you are a bad speller. Although some find it easier than others, spelling is a skill that can be learned. The fun tests in this book will give you lots of spelling practice. There are also guidelines to help you avoid making mistakes.

User's guide

Each double page in this section focuses on particular spelling problems. Read through the summary of guidelines at the top of each left-hand page, then test your spelling by trying the puzzles which follow. The book has not been designed for writing in, so you will need some paper and a pencil or pen for jotting down your answers. You can check them on pages 28-32. Don't worry if you make mistakes. Just work through the book, then go back to the start and try again. You will definitely improve next time.

Watch out for boxes like this. These contain words for you to learn and test yourself on. Some will be new to you, so have a dictionary handy to check up on what they mean and how to use them.

Why is good spelling necessary?

Spelling is an important skill for many reasons. Above all, it is vital to be able to spell correctly so that you do not confuse your reader. For instance, there are certain words (called homophones) which sound the same, but which have different spellings and meanings.

The cereal was advertised on television.

The serial was advertised on television.

Other spellings are so similar that even a small mistake may make it difficult for your reader to understand you.

The desert was a generous helping of lemon meringue pie.

The dessert was a generous helping of lemon meringue pie.

As your spelling gets better, your writing style will also improve, because you will be able to write with confidence, using a wide range of words to express yourself.

Where does English spelling come from?

Modern English is a mixture of languages. Long ago, the Ancient Britons spoke Celtic, but over the centuries each of the peoples that invaded Britain contributed words from their own languages. For example, *skirt* comes from Old Norse, *index* from Latin, and *garage* from French. More recently, English has been affected by influences such as the growth of travel and trade, the World Wars and the rise of broadcasting. For instance, did you know that the word *shampoo* comes from India, *studio* from Italy, and *parade* from Spain? English is still changing today, in order to express new ideas and experiences.

USEFUL TERMS
What are vowels?

The five letters *a*, *e*, *i*, *o* and *u* are known as vowels. When *y* sounds like "i" (as in *sky*) or "e" (as in *jolly*), it is also considered to be a vowel. The other letters of the alphabet, including *y* as it sounds in *yes*, are called consonants. Each vowel has two sounds: short and long. Say the words below. The top line has short vowel sounds. The bottom line has long vowel sounds.

hat   fence   stick   dog   mud

gate   tree   kite   bone   blue

What are syllables?

Many words have more than one vowel sound. Each part of a word which has a separate vowel sound is called a syllable. For example, *dig* has one syllable, *mar/ket* has two syllables, *ex/pen/sive* has three and *in/vis/ib/le* has four. Breaking a word down into syllables often makes spelling easier.

Try counting the syllables in the words on this shopping list, then check your answers with the ones on page 28. Don't look at the number of vowels in each word, as this can be misleading. Just say each word aloud, and count the vowel sounds you hear.

soap
toothpaste
detergent
bread
peanuts
macaroni
coffee
milk
eggs

honey
lemonade
cheese
tomatoes
cauliflower
onions
bananas
oranges

What is stress?

When you say words of more than one syllable, you usually put more emphasis on one syllable than the others. For example, *market*, *invisible*, *expensive*. This emphasis is called stress, or accent.

Read out the words on the shopping list again. Can you hear where the stress lies in each one? Check your answers on page 28.

Check your answers on page 28.

What makes a spelling correct?

The idea of "correct" spelling is not very old. Until the 18th century, people spelled words however they liked. They even thought nothing of spelling a word in several different ways in the same piece of writing. When the invention of the printing press made written material available to large numbers of people, it became clear that spelling needed to be standardized, so everyone knew exactly what a writer meant. The first English dictionary was written by Samuel Johnson and published in 1755. But the patterns he defined were not always consistent or logical. So today some words are more difficult to spell than others.

English has continued to change since then, as new words have entered the language and others have dropped out of use. Also, the spelling, pronunciation and meaning of some words have gradually altered. This is why there are differences between British, American and Australian English. You will find that a few words can still be spelled in more than one way (such as gipsy/gypsy). In these cases, use the spelling you find easiest to remember. But if you are surprised by a spelling, always check it. It may be misspelled, or even be a different word. For example, passed and past do not mean the same thing.

3

Vowel sounds are often spelled in unexpected ways. For example, a long "e" is spelled by *i* in *margarine*, but by *y* in *tiny*. Also, many vowel sounds are spelled by two vowels together. For example, *tread* (short "e" spelled *ea*) or *float* (long "o" spelled *oa*). The most common ways of spelling vowel sounds are set out for you here. Look at these examples, then test yourself on the puzzles. You can find the answers on page 28.

a **short** *cat*
long *plate   paid   may*
steak   weight
prey   gauge

e **short** *set   dead*
long *eat   very   demon*
feel   sardine
piece   ceiling

u **short** *duck   come   young*
long *clue   food   prune*
fruit   screw   do
coupon

o **short** *pop   wasp   laurel   cough*
long *stone   soap   toe   throw*

i **short** *fit   syrup   build*
long *pie   lime   sky   height*

An eye for an *i*

Only a few words end in *i*. These are mostly from other languages. Can you spell some from the clues below? The first letter of each word is given to help you.

1	Two piece swimsuit	B
2	Trip to see animals in the wild	S
3	Thrown at weddings	C
4	Writing and drawings on public walls	G
5	Car with driver	T
6	Long, thin pasta	S
7	Snow-sport footwear	S
8	Short skirt	M
9	Yellow-brown shade	K
10	Type of spicy sausage	S

Double trouble

Can you guess the half-spelled words in these speech bubbles? Two vowels are missing from each gap.

What b_utiful w_ther!

P_ple confuse us bec_se we're so alike.

I h_rd it'll cl_d over and r_n later tod_.

Your barg_n bl_ j_ns r_lly s_t you.

I've b_n w_ting an h_r for my fr_nd.

I s_d we'd l_ve at the us_l time.

Pl_se can we l_k ar_nd ag_n first?

──One vowel short──

Which vowel is missing from each of these limericks?

There _nce was a man with the n_ti_n,
T_ live _n a b_at _n the _cean,
But his p__r little daughter,
Quite hated the water,
Because _f the up and d_wn m_ti_n.

1

There was an old woman from B_te,
Who played o_t of t_ne on the fl_te,
The noise was so bad
That it drove her q_ite mad
And left her _nable to toot.

2

There once w_s _ brown cow n_med D_isy,
Who w_s pretty but tot_lly l_zy,
She'd gr_ze in her field,
But no milk would she yield,
_nd this drove the f_rmer quite cr_zy.

3

There was a young woman named Lizz_.
Who kept feeling terribl_ dizz_,
She consulted a doctor,
But he onl_ mocked her,
And said that he found it a m_ster_.

4

There was a young g_rl from Tyree,
Who couldn't count further than three,
She tr_ed and she tr_ed -
But _n va_n. "Oh," she cr_ed,
"Four, f_ve, s_x, _s the problem, you see."

5

Th_r_ onc_ was a young boy named Mik_,
Who rod_ a long way on a bik_,
His l_gs got so sor_,
H_ could cycl_ no mor_.
So inst_ad had to g_t off and hik_.

6

──Silent e──

Some words end in an *e* which you do not pronounce (such as sam**e**, concret**e** and arriv**e**). This silent *e* is important because it gives a long sound to the vowel that comes before it. For example, if you add a silent *e* to the ends of *hat*, *bit* and *pet*, they become *hate*, *bite* and *Pete*.

1 Take the silent *e* off each word below. Which words have you now spelled? Do these new words have short or long vowel sounds?

use	note	fate	spite	made
hope	rate	kite	cute	ripe

2 Now add a silent *e* onto these words, and listen how the sound of each one changes.

bar	rag	hug	car	fir
sag	far	par	wag	her

3 Which vowel is missing from each of these words? Do they have short or long vowel sounds?

Chin_se	sh_pe	wh_te	teleph_ne
conf_se	al_ne	prod_ce	al_ve
supp_se	compl_te	esc_pe	h_me
resc_e	comb_ne	b_the	appet_te
celebr_te	am_se	sev_re	supr_me

Here are some words in which the letter *y* acts as a vowel. First, use a dictionary to check any meanings you aren't sure of. Next, test your spelling by reading, covering, then writing each word.

TIDY	LYRIC	STYLE
GOODBYE	DYNAMITE	TYPICAL
SYSTEM	CYCLE	SATISFY
DRY	EYE	BUTTERFLY
HYSTERICAL	CAPACITY	RHYTHM
LYNCH	SYMMETRY	DYNASTY
MERCY	TYRANNY	NYLON
GYMNASIUM	HYPNOTIZE	APPLY
MYTHOLOGY	NAVY	OCCUPY
CYMBALS	SUPPLY	SYRINGE
PYTHON	READY	SHY
SYMPHONY	TYRANT	DYING
EMERGENCY	HYMN	UNITY
CRYSTAL	LUXURY	RHYME
TYPEWRITER	PRETTY	LYNX
PYRAMID	CENTURY	SYNTHETIC
ANONYMOUS	IDYLLIC	TYCOON

The most usual way to make a singular noun (naming word) plural is to add an *s*. For example, *word/words.* But there are some other ways of making plurals which are explained below.

You should NEVER use an apostrophe (') to make a word plural. Apostrophes show the owner of something (such as *my daughter's books*). They also mark missing letters. For example, the *o* in *are not* is replaced by an apostrophe in *aren't*.

ies If a noun ends in *y*, look at the letter before the *y*. If it is a vowel, just add an *s* (as in *monkey/monkeys*). If it is a consonant, change *y* to *i* and add *es* (as in *baby/babies*).

ves To form the plurals of nouns ending in *ff*, add an *s* (as in *cuffs, cliffs*). But for words ending in *f* or *fe*, change the *f* or *fe* to *v* and add *es* (as in *sheaf/sheaves, knife/knives*). Exceptions are: *dwarfs, chiefs, griefs, roofs, proofs, beliefs* and *safes.* Four words can have either spelling: *wharfs/wharves, hoofs/hooves, turfs/turves, scarfs/scarves.*

es To make the plural of nouns which end in *ch, sh, s, ss, x* or *z*, simply add *es*. For example, *torches, dishes, buses, kisses, boxes* and *waltzes.*

oes To make the plural of words ending in *o*, add *s* if there is a vowel before the final *o* (as in *zoo*) or if the word is to do with music (such as *solo* and *soprano*). Also add *s* to *disco* and *photo* (*discos, photos*) and names of peoples, such as *Filipinos*. But when there is a consonant before the final *o* (and the words do not fall into the above categories), add *es*. For example, *potatoes.*

Spies in the skies

Key:
1: s
2: ies

Two rival organizations have given their secret agents passwords which end in *y*. One organization's passwords can be made plural by adding an *s*, while the passwords of the other change to *ies*. The agents cannot work out who belongs to which organization. Can you help them by sorting out the passwords into two lists?

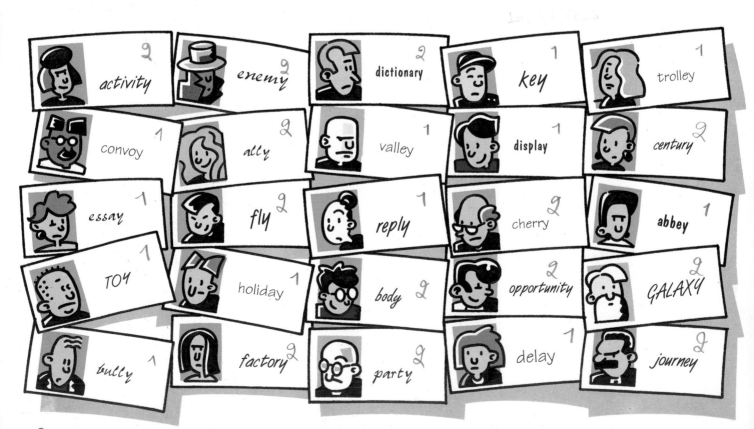

O! What now?

Words which end in *o* have been replaced in this poem with pictures. Can you spell the plurals of these things?

IF I WERE A MARTIAN AND I LIVED IN OUTER SPACE
I'D LIKE TO VISIT EARTH ONE DAY AND LOOK AROUND THE PLACE

I'D LIKE TO MEET AN ⬚ AND VISIT HIS ⬚

THEN TRAVEL TO AUSTRALIA TO SEE A ⬚

I'D ROAM THE VAST AND GRASSY PLAINS TO FIND THE ⬚

AND TREMBLE AT THE BOTTOM OF A FIERY ⬚

I'D SUFFER FROM ⬚ BITES IN HOT EXOTIC LANDS

AND I'D LEARN TO PLAY ⬚ AND I'D MARCH WITH BIG BRASS BANDS

I'D HAVE A LITTLE VEGETABLE PATCH WHERE I COULD DIG AND SOW

THEN WATCH ⬚ AND ⬚ PLANTS TAKE ROOT AND GROW

AND JUST IN CASE ONE DAY I SHOULD FORGET THE THINGS I'D DONE

I'D BE SURE TO TAKE A ⬚ OF EACH AND EVERY ONE

SO WHEN THE TIME CAME TO RETURN TO WORK ON MY SPACE-STATION
I SHOULD ALWAYS HAVE THESE SOUVENIRS OF MY EARTHLY VACATION

F words

In these sentences, words ending in *f*, *fe* and *ff* are singular, but should be plural. Can you spell their plural forms correctly?

1 It took him three puff to blow out the candles on his birthday cake.
2 "Put on scarf, take handkerchief, and behave yourself," their mother said.
3 The hoof of the galloping horses thundered over the race course.
4 Deciduous trees shed their leaf every year.
5 The team played badly in both half of the match.
6 The thief blew open all the safe and escaped with treasures worth millions.
7 It is said that cats have nine life.
8 The shelf were stacked with loaf of bread of all shapes and sizes.
9 At night in the mountains, they could hear wolf howling.
10 King Henry VIII had six wife.
11 Houses in hot countries often have flat sun-roof.

Singularly confused

Words that were originally from other languages often have strange plurals. Do you know how to spell the plurals of the red words in these sentences?

1 I fell asleep on the bus and ended up at the terminus.
2 In the basket of mushrooms I had picked was a poisonous fungus.
3 Another name for a grub that turns into an insect is a larva.
4 My birthday cake was a huge, creamy, chocolate gateau.
5 I looked at the exam paper, and realized we had been taught the wrong syllabus.
6 CO_2 is the chemical formula for carbon dioxide.
7 The worst thing to do in a crisis is panic.
8 People's lives can be changed by the medium of television.

Plural puzzler

There are a few words which have irregular plurals. For example, one *louse* becomes several *lice*. How many other irregular plurals do you know?

Some nouns, such as *sheep*, stay the same in both the singular and plural. How many more words can you think of like this?

Most sounds in English can be spelled in more than one way. So choosing the right spelling for a particular word can be confusing.

k The sound "k" as in *kid* is sometimes known as hard *c*. It can be spelled as in **c**at, **k**i**ck**, a**cc**ordion, e**ch**o and grotes**que**.

air The sound "air" can be spelled as in ch**air**, sh**are**, b**ear**, th**ere**, th**eir**, and **aer**ial.

sh "sh" sounds can be spelled as in **s**ure, ru**sh**, op**t**ion, i**ss**ue, so**c**ial, an**x**ious and **ch**ef.

shun A "shun" sound is mostly spelled as in ac**tion**, man**sion**, mi**ssion**, or comple**xion**. But watch out for cu**shion**, fa**shion**, o**cean**, musi**cian** and suspi**cion**.

zhun "zhun" sound is always spelled **sion** (as in occa**sion**), except in words which describe nationality. In these words, "zhun" is spelled **sian** (as in *Asian*, *Malaysian*, *Polynesian*).

er/uh The ends of many English words aren't stressed, so differences between them can be hard to hear. For example, the final syllables of the words farm**er**, simil**ar**, came**ra**, theat**re** and act**or** just sound like "er" or "uh". The sound "er" also occurs in the middle of words. In these cases, it can be spelled as in s**er**ve, **ear**th, b**ir**d, w**or**d, p**ur**se, j**our**ney or Febru**ar**y.

——— **Conquer kicking *k*** ———

Kevin spells all "k" sounds with only the letter *k*. Can you correct his spelling?

I like

Snakes and krokodiles   Hearing my voice eko

Pikniking in the park   Books about shipwreks   Doing magik triks

Klimbing trees

I dislike

Akting in skool plays   Singing in the koir

Losing my train tiket   Stomak ake   Kornflakes, chiken and brokoli

Kemistry lessons

——— **Are you an *air*-head** ———

There are eleven spelling mistakes in this letter. Can you spot them?

Dear Gran

My first time on an ereoplane was really exciting - when I'm a millionair I'm going to have my own private jet. My suitcase was bulging - Dad says I'll never have time to where all the clothes and pears of shoes I've brought. But I still managed to forget my hare brush, and Sue's forgotten her teddy bare.

We've got a lovely room to shair that looks out on the sea - their are some rair birds to spot along this part of the coast. We're going to a funfare tomorrow.

Take cair - we'll see you soon,

Love

Donna XXXXXXX

Er ...? Uh ...?

Forgetful Rachel has written two lists to help her remember things. But she has forgotten how to spell "er" and "uh" sounds. Which letters are missing?

THINGS TO BUY:

pizz_, sug_, butt_,

fl_r, tun_, banan_s,

hamburg_s, marm_lade,

chocolate flav_ milkshake,

writing pap_ and env_lopes,

an eras_, a rul_ and a pair

of sciss_s,

2 met_s of p_ple ribbon,

film for my camer_,

a packet of cake mixt_e,

a batt_y for my calculat_,

a b_thday present

for Samanth_

Rememb_ to take my p_se!

THINGS TO DO:

1 Cut out some pict_es of famous act_s for my project.

2 Sign up for the class trip to the theat_.

3 Ask my next-door neighb_ if I can look for my basketball in his garden.

4 See if my sist_ will let me wear her new dress on Sat_day.

5 Remind Amand_ that it's our t_n this week to look after the _thw_ms in the science room. (Yuk!)

Be sure of *sh*, *shun* and *zhun*

Can you complete this newspaper article by spelling a "sh", "shun" or "zhun" sound to replace each numbered gap?

TRAIN CRASH AND CARRY!

There was a colli..1.. at Spellham Station this morning between two express trains. An electri..2.. carried out an investiga..3.. and reported that an explo..4.. had destroyed signals at a junc..5.. down the line. No one was hurt, but in the confu..6.. two bags of ca..7.. were stolen from one of the trains. The police are an..8..ous to solve this crime quickly, and are appealing for informa..9.. . They have i..10..ued a descrip..11.. of two men seen earlier on the platform, who are now under suspi..12.. . One has a mousta..13..e and was disguised as a railway offi..14..al. The other had a worried expre..15.. and a bag with the ini..16..als S.H. on it. They both left together in a ..17..auffeur-driven car.

You will almost certainly have seen words spelled with letters that you don't pronounce. These are often letters that used to be pronounced in Old English. For instance, before the 10th century, the *k* in *knot*, the *g* in *gnaw* and the *l* in *folk* were all pronounced. Over the years, the pronunciation of some words changed, while their spellings stayed the same.

So some letters became silent. Other silent letters, such as the *b* in *doubt* and the *p* in *receipt*, were deliberately added during the Renaissance by English scholars. They were trying to make certain words look more like the Latin words they had originally come from.

Here are some common silent letters, showing when they occur:

b "silent" b sometimes occurs after *m* at the end of a syllable or word (as in *plumber* or *climb*). It is also found in *debt*, *doubt*, *subtle*.

c can be silent after *s* (as in *science* and *scent*).

k before *n* (as in *knife*, *knot* and *knitting*).

g often comes before *n* (as in *gnome* and *sign*).

h can follow w (as in *wheel*), g (as in *ghostly*), and r (as in *rhinoceros*). It is also found at the start of a word (as in *honour*), between vowels (as in *vehicle*), and after *x*, as in *exhibit*.

l is sometimes silent before d, k or m (as in *should*, *walk* or *salmon*).

n can be silent after *m* (as in *hymn*).

w is sometimes silent in front of *h* (as in *who*) and also before *r* at the start of a word (as in *wrath* and *wreck*).

p is silent before *s*, *n* or *t* in words which come from Greek (such as *pneumatic*). It can also be silent after *s*, as in *raspberry*.

s silent in *island*, *isle*, *aisle*.

t is sometimes silent after *s* (as in *fasten*).

Tongue twister teasers

Which silent letter is missing from each of these nonsense tongue twisters?

How quickly can you say each one?

1. We wish we were w_ispering w_ales in w_ite w_irling waters.

2. _nomes, _nats and _nus all _nash and _naw _narled nutshells.

3. Fo_k wa_k cha_ky paths ca_mly sta_king quiet qua_mless sa_mon.

4. The _night who _new the _nack of _nitting _nots _nelt with a _nobbly _napsack on the _noll.

5. The clim_ing plum_er's thum_ grew num_.

6. R_yming, r_ythmical r_inoceroses like r_ine- stones and r_ubarb.

7. The _retched _riter _reaked his _rath by _renching the _rinkled _rappers from the _recked _ristwatches.

8. Around the solem_ colum_s the singers' hym_s condem_ed the Autum_.

9. G_ostly g_ouls and g_astly g_osts eat g_erkins in g_oulish g_ettos.

Conversation clues

Which silent letters are missing from the words in these speech bubbles?

W..1..at have you been up to?

Last week I had my pa..2..m read by Madame Rippemovsky, the famous ..3..sychic. I was ag..4..ast at the things she ..5..new. She told me all about my "keep the countryside tidy" campai..6..n, also that I don't like lam..7.. chops or egg yo..8..k, and that ras..9..berries are the fruit I like most. She ..10..new that I want to be a fashion desi..11..ner and that I'd seen an art ex..12..ibition the day before. She told me that I shou..13..d look for my lost s..14..issors in my brown bag, and also that one day I wou..15..d sail on a ya..16..17..t around forei..18..n and exotic i..19..lands with a tall, dark and han..20..some stranger! I hope she's ri..21..22..t!

Hear this

Certain words have letters which some people pronounce, but others don't, such as the *o* in *factory*. See if you can guess a few of them from these clues. The first letter of each is given to help you. Which are the letters that are often silent?

1	Potatoes, carrots, peas...	V
2	The month after January	F
3	A small-scale copy or model	M
4	Another word for precious	V
5	The one after eleventh	T
6	Sweet brown or white confectionery	C
7	Fahrenheit or Celsius	T

8	UK politicians assemble here	P
9	Machine for sucking up dust	V
10	This means out of the ordinary	E
11	Custer was a famous one	G
12	A jewel	D
13	Home for monks	M
14	The day after Tuesday	W

The sound of silence

Can you unscramble the jumbled names of the things pictured here?

There is at least one silent letter in each word. Can you spot them?

1 mobb
2 porbucad
3 nydhig
4 strewrel
5 kenrock
6 ceetrip
7 bruscm
8 oybu
9 fenik
10 stacel

Some letters regularly occur together in combination. But this can be confusing, as one combination of letters can spell different sounds, while a single sound may be spelled by more than one combination.

gh Combinations such as *ough*, *augh*, and *igh* can be tricky, as the *gh* is heard either as "f" (as in *tough*), or is silent (as in *light*). The most difficult is *ough*, as several sounds are spelled this way.

dge A "j" sound at the end of a word or syllable is spelled *ge* if the vowel sound is long (as in *huge*), or when there is a short vowel with a consonant (as in *cringe*). But if there is a short vowel and no consonant, use *dge* (as in *dredge*). An exception to remember is *pigeon*.

qu After the Norman Conquest, French scribes changed the Old English spelling *cw* to *qu*. For example, *cwic* and *cwen* became *quick* and *queen*. Also, in a few words, they spelled a "k" sound with *que*, as in *picturesque*.

tch Watch out for "ch" sounds at the ends of words or syllables. Where there is a short vowel and no consonant, "ch" is spelled *tch*, as in *catch*. The most common exceptions are: *such*, *much*, *attach*, *detach*, *sandwich* and *bachelor*.

Qu quiz

The king can only reach the queen to deliver his bouquet if he can answer these clues correctly. Can you help him? Begin at number one, and find a word that includes *qu* for each clue. The first letter of each word is given in red.

1. OFTEN, OR MANY TIMES F
2. NOT SEE-THROUGH O
3. A SMALL NUT-EATING ANIMAL S
4. TO GIVE IN OR TO GIVE UP Q
5. PEACEFUL OR CALM T
6. WHERE GOLDFISH ARE KEPT A
7. A FOURTH OF SOMETHING Q
8. AN OPEN TIED UP Q
9. ORIGINAL OR ONE OF A KIND U
10. FOUR-SIDED SHAPE S
11. FAST Q
12. WILLIAM THE ...C
13. WHERE BOATS ARE
14. AMOUNT Q
15. WASTE MONEY S
16. A WATER-CARRYING BRIDGE A
17. ARGUMENT Q
18. A GROUP OF 4 Q
19. STRANGE Q
20. A KING'S WIFE Q

Do you know what all these *qu* words mean? Test your spelling by reading, covering, then writing each one.

QUADRUPED
LACQUER
ACQUIRE
SQUASH
GROTESQUE
QUOTA
ETIQUETTE
QUALIFICATION
QUINTET
EQUILIBRIUM
QUOTATION
MARQUEE
QUALM
INQUISITIVE
QUILL
ACQUAINTANCE
QUEUE
REQUISITION
QUERY
EQUATION
QUINTESSENTIAL
QUALITY
SQUADRON
REQUEST

---ge or dge?---

The sound "j" is missing from the gaps here. Can you pick the right spelling for each one?

---choose *ch* or *tch*---

You can complete the article below by replacing each gap with either *ch* or *tch*.

Pet show fiasco

A colle..1.. pet show ended in disaster last week. Besides the usual cats and dogs, some rather stran..2.. entrants emer..3..d, including a he..4..hog, a ba..5..r, and a rock in a ca..6..! The ju..7.. (Annie Mall, a local vet) crin..8..d as a cat ate a mouse called Mi..9..t, and a parrot mana..10..d to fly up to a high le..11.., out of reach. Some people began to fi..12..t, and accused the he..13..hog of having fleas. Its angry owner said that such remarks did dreadful dama..14.. to people's ima..15.. of the creatures, and blows were exchan..16..d. In the confusion, a puppy called Smu..17.. ran off with the ba..18.. for first prize, and was later declared the winner.

Ki..1..en Pun..2..-up!

Guests at a local hotel had only sandwi..3..es for lun..4.. today, as chefs Pierre Noir (Fren..5..) and Jan Van Glyk (Du..6..) were fighting. Noir accused Van Glyk of scor..7..ing his ..8..icken dish by swi..9..ing up the oven. Van Glyk said he hadn't tou..10..ed it and Noir was no ma..11.. for him anyway. The waiters wa..12..ed and ..13..eered as Noir ..14..ased Van Glyk, clu..15..ing a bu..16..er's ha..17..et. Van Glyk threw a ba..18.. of eggs at Noir, who then poured ke..19..up over Van Glyk's head. The enraged Van Glyk pun..20..ed Noir, who fell and hit his head on a ben..21.., while Van Glyk pi..22..ed forward, wren..23..ing his ankle. Both needed to be carried on a stre..24..er to an ambulance. The police fe..25..ed them from the hospital, where Noir received ten sti..26..es, and Van Glyk, a pair of cru..27..es.

---The *gh* trap---

The combinations *ough*, *augh* and *igh* are missing from these speech bubbles. But which fits each gap?

13

A prefix is a group of letters (such as *inter* or *sub*) which you add onto the beginning of a word to change its meaning. Adding a prefix is quite straightforward - you usually keep all the letters, even if the two you are joining are the same. For example, *dis + satisfied = dissatisfied*, *un + nerve = unnerve*.

But when *all* and *well* are used as prefixes, one *l* is dropped. For example, *all + ways = always*, *well + fare = welfare*. But do not drop an *l* when *well* is used with a hyphen. For example, *well-made* and *well-off*. On these pages you can test yourself on some of the most common prefixes.

Guesswork

Most prefixes come from Latin, Greek and Old English. Knowing what they mean can often help you guess the meaning of a new word. Can you work out the meaning of each prefix below by looking at the examples?

trans	transplant	transform	transfusion
re	replace	reunion	recapture
hyper	hypersensitive	hypermarket	hyperactive
post	postpone	postnatal	postgraduate
micro	microchip	microwave	microscope
circum	circumference	circumnavigate	circumstance
omni	omnipotent	omnivore	omnibus
auto	autobiography	autopilot	automatic
multi	multinational	multimillionaire	multilateral
photo	photograph	photosynthesis	photosensitive
anti	anticlimax	antifreeze	antihero
pre	prehistoric	prejudge	prepayment
extra	extraterrestrial	extrasensory	extraordinary
mono	monorail	monopoly	monologue

Picture this

Use the picture clues to guess the prefixes missing from the words below.

1 -pede

2 -scope

3 -circular

4 -natural

5 -happy

6 -cycle

7 -sphere

8 -national

9 -angles

10 -marine

Singled out

Here are some less common prefixes and their meanings:

Do you know what the following words mean?

ante	before/in front of	**1**	**antenatal**
ultra	extreme/beyond	**2**	**ultramodern**
pseudo	false	**3**	**pseudonym**
demi	half	**4**	**demigod**
homo	the same/like	**5**	**homophones**
intra	inside/within	**6**	**intravenous**
mega	large/great	**7**	**megastar**
hypo	too little	**8**	**hypothermia**
arch	chief	**9**	**archbishop**

Matching pairs

Can you make words which match the numbered descriptions by joining the prefixes and words below?

1 below freezing
2 junction
3 below the earth
4 naughtiness
5 not usual
6 deceitful
7 against the law
8 above the ground floor
9 not to be relied upon
10 to come back again
11 to overcome something
12 action to avoid danger
13 happening twice a year
14 too many to count

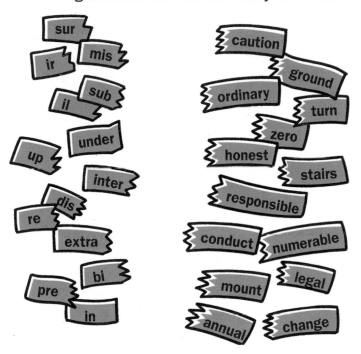

sur ir mis il sub up under dis re inter extra bi pre in

caution ground ordinary turn zero honest stairs responsible conduct numerable mount legal annual change

Precise prefixes

Try replacing each of these descriptions with a word that begins with a prefix.

1 lots of different shades
2 to put off until later
3 a self-written life story
4 fluent in two languages
5 an advance showing
6 not cooked enough
7 to vanish
8 to translate a secret message
9 forever
10 to seek out information
11 a disappointing ending
12 not contented
13 unchanging level of sound
14 to change drastically
15 flawed

Face the opposition

Try forming the opposites of the words in capitals below by adding either *un, il, im, mis, in, ir,* or *dis* onto the front of them.

"How dare you OBEY me!" the king shouted.

Cruelty to animals is completely NECESSARY.

Her writing was so bad it was LEGIBLE.

The 16th century vase I had smashed was REPLACEABLE.

Cats have very DEPENDENT natures.

It is very PROBABLE that we will have snow in August.

Drugs are LEGAL in most countries.

Due to our CALCULATIONS, the carpet was the wrong size.

I could see by the scowl on her face that she APPROVED.

At present, it is POSSIBLE for men to have babies.

"Hurry up! We haven't got all day," she yelled PATIENTLY.

To waste paper is to be environmentally RESPONSIBLE.

We had the FORTUNE to miss each other at the airport.

Although he regretted it, his decision was REVERSIBLE.

In both looks and personality, the twins were SIMILAR.

The MANAGEABLE children ran riot in the classroom.

I used to be DECISIVE, but now I'm not so sure.

It is POLITE to open your mouth while chewing your food.

15

Soft c

An "s" sound before *i, y* or *e* can be spelled with a soft *c*, as in *concept*, *cylinder* and *circumstance*. If a word finishes with a long vowel or a consonant followed by an "s" sound, it is often spelled *ce* (as in *trace* and *innocence*). By contrast, *se* at the end of a word usually spells a "z" sound (as in *exercise*).
* Exceptions include *tense, precise, collapse, expense, immense, response, suspense* and *sense*.

Hard g

A "g" as it sounds in *green* is known as hard *g*. In certain words, the letter *u* separates a hard *g* from *e* or *i* (as in *guest* and *guide*). Sometimes *u* also separates a hard *g* and the letter *a* (as in *guarantee* and *guard*). Certain words end with a hard *g* spelled *gue* (for example, *fatigue, rogue* and *league*).

Soft g

The sound "j" before *e, i* or *y* can be spelled with a soft *g*, as in *gentle*, *ginger* and *gymnastics*. At the ends of words, the sound "jee" is spelled *gy* (as in *biology*) and the sound "idj" is spelled *age* (as in *manage*). *Acknowledge, porridge* and *college* are the most common exceptions to remember.

Endings

Here is a rule for adding endings to words which finish in soft *c* or *g* followed by *e* (such as *face* and *stage*). Drop the final *e* if the ending starts with a vowel (*stage* + *ing* + *staging*), but keep it if the ending starts with a consonant (*face* + *less* = *faceless*). But when adding *ous*, keep *e* after soft *g* (*courage* + *ous* + *courageous*), and change it to *i* after soft *c* (*grace* + *ous* = *gracious*). Also keep the *e* when adding *able* (as in *peace* + *able* = *peaceable*).

Get guessing

Meet private investigator Guy Roper. He puts words containing hard *g* sounds into code. Can you crack it?

Did you 7, 21, 5, 19, 19 it was me?
I'm so good at 4, 9, 19, 7, 21, 9, 19, 9, 14, 7 myself that even my 3, 15, 12, 12, 5, 1, 7, 21, 5, 19 don't recognize me. I 7, 21, 1, 18, 1, 14, 20, 5, 5 I'll solve any mystery, however 9, 14, 20, 18, 9, 7, 21, 9, 14, 7 it is. If you know where to look, you can always find clues to 7, 21, 9, 4, 5 you to a 7, 21, 9, 12, 20, 25 person.
At the moment, I'm undercover as a musician - that's why I've got a 7, 21, 9, 20, 1, 18. But unluckily musical notes are a foreign 12, 1, 14, 7, 21, 1, 7, 5 to me. I have to be on my 7, 21, 1, 18, 4 all the time so I don't blow my cover.
Shhhh! Someone's coming.
I'd better 7, 5, 20 away ...

Putting an end to it

Can you add endings to the words in capitals, so that the sentences read properly? Make any spelling changes you think are necessary to alter each word correctly.

1 Gandhi was a PEACE man.
2 I'm no good at SLICE cake.
3 Our new house is very SPACE.
4 His suitcase was UNMANAGE.
5 Designer clothes are OUTRAGE expensive.
6 I like hot and SPICE curries.
7 Bright red is very NOTICE.
8 Small oranges are JUICE.
9 He GLANCE around nervously.
10 The bull was CHARGE at me.
11 His JUDGE was too harsh.
12 The stain is SCARCE visible.
13 Tap DANCE is fun.
14 Fire-fighters are COURAGE.
15 Try BALANCE on one leg.
16 It is ADVANTAGE to speak several languages.

*Turn to pages 26-27 to find out about certain words which end in *ce* when they are nouns, and *se* when they are verbs.

Do you get the gist?

Use these clues to guess words with a soft *g*. The first letter of each is given for you.

1   The study of the Earth, its climate, and how people live   G
2   An animal with a long neck   G
3   A likeness of something or someone, perhaps in a mirror   I
4   Bacteria which make you ill   G
5   Dull, dismal or dirty   D
6   Where a car is kept overnight   G
7   A line down the left side of paper   M
8   Starting point, or beginning   O

9   You give someone this when you say sorry to them   A
10   This is in the air you breathe   O
11   What you might call a person selfish with money   S
12   A very tall person   G
13   Used for binding up injuries   B
14   Fierce, wild or primitive   S
15   A very intelligent person   G
16   Wire enclosure for animals   C

Spell soft *c*

In these three advertisements, words with soft *c* have been jumbled up. Can you unscramble them?

1

Crunch-U-Like

Try our new raceel!

WE GUARANTEE YOU'LL LOVE OUR CIPEER OF
**crunchy oats and
ciyuj stuirc fruit chunks**
OR YOUR MONEY BACK!

2

MERRIMAN'S CUCSIR

OPENS AT 8PM WITH A
**FACEMINTGIN SICNOSROPE
GAZE AT THE**
INOSECRIP OF KNIFE-THROWERS
THE NICETRATNOONC OF JUGGLERS
THE CRAGE OF TRAPEZE-ARTISTS
THE BLANECA OF HIGH-WIRE
WALKERS
GASP IN ECMINXTEET
AS STEVIE STAR SPINS TWO HUNDRED ASCURSE
AND
MARVIN THE MARVELLOUS STINYCUILC
MAKES A STEEP ACNEST UP A TIGHTROPE
LAUGH AT THE ENEXTCELL CLOWNS!
BE DEEDVICE BY THE WORLD-FAMOUS MAGICIAN
"THE GREAT MYSTERIO"
SEE THE GREATEST SHOW OF THE TUNRYCE!

3

Sample the ceepa
of
Writington Nature Reserve

A brief film-show in our mini-minace rotnudesic
the many different sicpees you can see.

Wander around our curralic nature trail
at your own novinecenec.

Don't forget to visit the swannery, where you can
watch gsnecty and parent swans in their natural habitat

WHY NOT STOP FOR REFRESHMENT AT OUR SELF-VEERSIC CAFE?
SEE YOU SOON!

The ends of many English words are not emphasized. This means that differences can be difficult to hear and so also to spell.

able/ible
The endings *able* and *ible* are often confused, as they both sound and mean the same (to be fit or able to). As *able* is much more common, it's easiest to learn which words end in *ible*. But there are some useful tips to remember.

You usually drop silent *e* when adding *able* or *ible*. For example, *use* + *able* = *usable*, *sense* + *ible* = *sensible*. But remember that after soft *c* or *g* there is an *e* before *able* (for example, *peaceable*, *manageable*), but not before *ible* (*invincible*, *unintelligible*). Also watch out for *soluble*, which has neither *a* nor *i*.

cul
Words which end in the sound "cul" are spelled *cal* if they are adjectives (such as *medical* and *practical*), *cle* if they are nouns (such as *circle*), and sometimes also *kle* (as in tickle and fickle).

ise/ize
You might see some words spelled both *ize* and *ise* (such as *realize* /*realise*). This is because in the UK both are correct in many cases. In the US, however, *ize* is the usual spelling. But in both countries there are some words which can only be spelled *ise*. These include: *advise*, *advertise*, *compromise*, *despise*, *devise*, *disguise*, *enterprise*, *exercise*, *improvise*, *revise*, *supervise*, *surmise*, *surprise*, *televise*. Also watch out for *prize* (a reward) and *prise* (to force something open).

ence/ance
More words end in *ence* or *ent* than *ance* or *ant*. After hard *c* or *g* use *ance*/*ant* (as in *significance*), but after a soft *c* or *g* use *ence*/*ent* (as in *negligent*). Watch out for *dependant* - this means a person who is *dependent*, with no *independence*.

---

w*ise* or w*ize*?

The "ize" sounds are missing from these sentences. But how should each one be spelled - *ise* or *ize*?

1 **She was so thin I hardly recogn_d her.**

2 **Exerc_ is good for you.**

3 **The second edition has been rev_d.**

4 **The teacher had 30 children to superv_.**

5 **My friends organ_d a surpr_ party for me.**

6 **The music shop special_s in pianos.**

7 **Some snakes hypnot_ their prey.**

8 **The sales assistant pressur_d me into buying it.**

9 **I won first pr_ in the competition.**

10 **Our new puppy was advert_d in the newspaper.**

11 **When the actor forgot his lines, he had to improv_.**

12 **I like taking part, but I desp_ losing.**

13 **My big brother critic_s me.**

14 **I went trick or treating disgu_d as a vampire.**

15 **I had to pr_ open the lid of the rusty old box.**

Probably horrible

Try replacing each numbered gap in this unusual report with either *able* or *ible*.

Last night, I was driving with the roof of my convert..1.. car down, when a strange light became vis..2.. in the sky. It landed in a nearby field, and I set off to investigate. As I drew nearer to the light, a spaceship became recogniz..3.. It wasn't advis..4.. to hang around, but I was unmov..5.. at the terr..6.. sight. Suddenly, a kind of collaps..7.. ladder appeared - whatever horr..8.. things were lurking inside wanted to be soci..9.. I didn't wait to find out if they were peace..10.., but ran for my life. It's understand..11.. if you find my incred..12.. story unbeliev..13.., as I have no reli..14.. proof. But I am sens..15.., respons..16.., and not at all gull..17... I never thought life in outer space was poss..18.., but this unforgett..19.. experience has made me change my mind.

Possibly problematical

The clues below describe words which end with a "cul" sound. The first letter of each word is given, to help you guess them. How is each word spelled?

1	What the p stands for in P.E	P
2	Round shape	C
3	Something in your way	O
4	Hanging finger of ice	I
5	Vegetables preserved in vinegar	P
6	Of utmost importance	C

7	Where your foot joins your leg	A
8	A type of music	C
9	Single eye glass	M
10	Cars, trucks etc. are all types of this	V
11	Two-wheeled transportation	B
12	In the surrounding area	L

Trail finder

The letters *a* and *e* are missing from the words in this grid. Starting at the top left arrow, there is an invisible path of *ant* and *ance* words through the surrounding *ent* and *ence* words, leading out at the bottom right arrow*. Can you find this path?

acquaint-nce		resid_nce			excell_nt		accid_nt
confid_nce	clear_nce	cli_nt	differ_nce	serv_nt	adjac_nt	inst_nt	sent_nce
differ_nce	allow_nce	evid_nt	griev_nce	appar_nt	import_nt	obedi_nt	fragr_nt
innoc_nt	ignor_nt	refer_nce	defend_nt	circumfer_nce	frequ_nt	pres_nce	reluct_nce
	sil_nt	ramp_nt			interfer_nce	persever_nce	
	occurr_nce	influ_nce	exist_nce	nuis_nce	impertin_nt	appear_nce	
intellig_nt	perman_nt	assist_nt	appli_nce	viol_nt	disturb_nce	promin_nt	consequ_nce
differ_nce	observ_nt	audi_nce	appar_nt	abs_nce	immin_nt	prud_nt	insol_nce
par_nt	dilig_nt	lieuten_nt	attend_nce	ten_nt	resembl_nce	insur_nce	pret_nce
conveni_nt		effici_nt			consci_nce		ambul_nce

Here are some words which end in *ible*. Do you know what they all mean?

Test your spelling by reading, covering, then writing each one.

EXHAUSTIBLE	CONTEMPTIBLE	IRRESISTIBLE	REVERSIBLE
NEGLIGIBLE	IMPERCEPTIBLE	OSTENSIBLE	PERMISSIBLE
INDIGESTIBLE	SUSCEPTIBLE	TANGIBLE	IMPOSSIBLE
DISCERNIBLE	FORCIBLE	INDESTRUCTIBLE	ACCESSIBLE
DIVISIBLE	EDIBLE	FLEXIBLE	INDELIBLE
LEGIBLE	PLAUSIBLE	INCORRIGIBLE	FEASIBLE
DISMISSIBLE	ELIGIBLE	ADMISSIBLE	FALLIBLE
REPREHENSIBLE	INCOMPREHENSIBLE	CORRUPTIBLE	DEDUCTIBLE

*The path can lead horizontally, vertically or diagonally.

A suffix is a letter, or combination of letters, added onto the end of a word to change either the meaning or the way the word is used. You usually need to make some alterations in order to add a suffix.

e If a word ends in silent *e*, drop the *e* when adding a suffix which begins with a vowel (for example, *examine* + *ation* = *examination*). But watch out for *age* + *ing*, as both *aging* and *ageing* are correct. Other exceptions include: *acreage*, *singeing*, *dyeing*, *gluey*, words to which *able* is added (such as *loveable*), and words ending in soft *c* or soft *g* when *ous* is added (see page 16).

If the suffix begins with a consonant, keep the *e* (for example, *care* + *less* = *careless*). Exceptions to this include: *argue* + *ment* = *argument*, *awe* + *ful* = *awful*, *due* + *ly* = *duly*, *true* + *ly* = *truly*, *whole* + *ly* = *wholly*.

ous The suffix *ous* means "full of" (for example, *generous* means "full of generosity"). When adding *ous* to words ending in *our*, such as *vigour*, you need to drop the *u* (*vigorous*). An extra *i* is needed in *laborious* (from *labour*). Also, a final *f* changes to *v* (*grief/grievous*).

y Many people find it confusing to add a suffix to a word ending in *y*. The rule is similar to the one for forming plurals (see page 6). Look at the letter before the *y*. If it is a vowel, just add the suffix. For example, *enjoy* + *ment* = *enjoyment*. If it is a consonant, change the *y* to *i*. For example, *luxury* + *ous* = *luxurious*, *heavy* + *ness* = *heaviness*, *plenty* + *ful* = *plentiful*.

But there are several exceptions to remember. Always keep a final *y* when adding *ing*. So *bury* + *ing* = *burying*, but *bury* + *ed* = *buried*. Also keep a final *y* before adding *ish* (as in *babyish*), and whenever the *y* sounds like long "i" (as in *shyly*). When adding the suffix *ous* to *pity*, *beauty* and *plenty*, you need to change the final *y* to *e*, not *i*, as in *piteous*, *beauteous* and *plenteous*. Also beware of another two exceptions: *joy* + *ous* = *joyous* and *calamity* + *ous* = *calamitous*. The letter *y* unexpectedly changes to *i* in the following: *lay/laid*, *pay/paid*, *say/said*, *slay/slain*, *day/daily*, *gay/gaily/gaiety*.

How about *ous*?

Try forming adjectives ending in *ous* from the nouns in capitals below.

1 Modelling is a GLAMOUR profession.

2 Lightning is extremely DANGER.

3 Japan is a very MOUNTAIN country.

4 I am reading a HUMOUR book.

5 Matthew is a STUDY pupil.

6 I am always ANXIETY to arrive on time.

7 Monkeys are MISCHIEF creatures.

8 Housework is dull and LABOUR.

9 A dancer's life demands RIGOUR discipline.

10 Be CAUTION when crossing the road.

Now you see it...

Sometimes a letter "disappears" when you add a suffix - usually a vowel in the last syllable. For example, *tiger + ess = tigress*. Try joining the words and suffixes opposite. You will need to make a letter disappear from each one. (Beware of numbers 8 and 10. You need to make an additional change to each of these.)

1	curious + ity	**9**	waiter + ess
2	hinder + ance	**10**	maintain + ance
3	repeat + ition	**11**	winter + y
4	exclaim + ation	**12**	explain + ation
5	disaster + ous	**13**	monster + ous
6	administer + ate	**14**	vain + ity
7	four + ty	**15**	remember + ance
8	pronounce + ation	**16**	nine + th

All's well that ends well

Can you add suffixes to the words in pink here, so that this letter makes sense? You will have to decide what to do with the silent *e* on the end of each word.

Dear Jamal

I'm WRITE to invite you to my birthday CELEBRATE next Thursday at the AMUSE park. It's still undergoing RENOVATE but will be open from Monday. It'll be very EXCITE. There's an AMAZE water-flume and a really SCARE roller-coaster. If you're EXTREME DARE, there's also a huge wheel in which you go backwards and upside down while REVOLVE sideways. Can you IMAGE it? Even I might not be ADVENTURE enough for that! Dad says he'll do the DRIVE, so don't have an ARGUE with your parents about how you're going to get there and back. I was USE at PERSUADE Dad to come in too. He thinks it'll be TIRE and NOISE. So, we can go on our own as long as we're on our best BEHAVE and act SENSE. Let me know if you're COME. I'm really HOPE to see you. It should be TRUE brilliant.

Lots of love
Miles

PS I'm sending INVITE to Tanya and Steve too, but it's LIKE Tanya won't come. She's quite NERVE and says you have to be RIDICULE to enjoy being frightened.

What to do with *y*

Follow these paths to find out which word leads to which suffix. Can you join them correctly? How many other ways can you find of joining these words and suffixes?

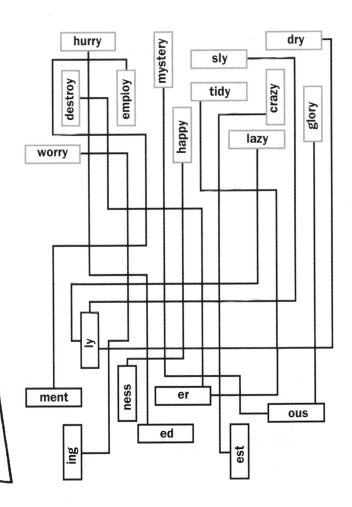

A real hand*ful*

When the word *full* is added as a prefix or suffix, it is spelled *ful*. For example, *full + ness = fulness, help + full = helpful*. But the suffix *fully* keeps the double *l*, as in *forgetfully* and *gracefully*.

Watch out for these special patterns:

*ski**ll***	*skilful, skilfully*
*wi**ll***	*wilful, wilfully*
*fi**ll***	*fulfil, fulfilment*
	(but *fulfilled* and *fulfilling*).

ie/ei Many people have problems spelling words which include *ie* or *ei*. Remembering this rhyme can be helpful:

> I BEFORE E EXCEPT AFTER C
> BUT ONLY WHERE THESE LETTERS
> SOUND LIKE LONG "E"

For example, the long "e" sound in *believe* is spelled *ie*, but this same sound is spelled *ei* in *perceive* as it occurs after the letter *c*.

There are some exceptions though, the most common of which are *seize*, *weird*, *caffeine*, *species* and *protein*.

But *ie* and *ei* sometimes make sounds other than long "e". For example, *ie* and *ei* can spell a long "i" sound (as in *society* and *height*). *Ei* can also spell a long "a" (as in *weight*), or the sound "air" (as in *their*). Watch out for tricky spellings like these.

---

i and *e* quick quiz

Use the picture clues to help you unscramble these words. Each one contains *ie* or *ei*.

1 ITHEF

2 HEGIT

3 WIVE

4 DIFLE

5 ITE

6 FRAKEHIDENCH

7 DILSHE

8 ROSELID

Here are some words which include ie and ei. Look them up in a dictionary if you don't know what they mean. Next, test your spelling by reading, covering, then writing each one.

SURFEIT	BELIEF	GAIETY	SIEGE
YIELD	EXPERIENCE	SKEIN	FEINT
RECEIPT	FREIGHT	DIESEL	LIEUTENANT
REIGN	CONCEIT	SIEVE	ACQUIESCE
MEDIEVAL	GRIEVANCE	RETRIEVE	BEIGE
LIE	PERCEIVE	SHEIK	CONSCIENCE
TIER	RELIEF	PIERCE	SERIES
EFFICIENT	WEIR	CEILING	THEIR
CONVENIENT	GEISHA	BIER	QUIET
RECIPIENT	MOVIES	ORIENTAL	RELIEVE
ATHEIST	EIDERDOWN	FIEND	ALIEN
SEISMIC	PIETY	SIENNA	DEITY

Missing pieces

Can you finish off these words correctly? They all include *ie* or *ei*.

1 Mrs Jones and Mrs Patel are next-door n_.
2 "Pat_ is a virtue," the p_ told his congregation.
3 The E_ Tower is in Paris.
4 Max is a very diso_ dog.
5 Pirates' gold is also known as "p_ of e_".
6 Santa Claus's s_ is drawn by seven r_.
7 When the portrait was unv_, they all saw it had gone!
8 He was h_ to the throne.

ei ie ei ie ei ie ei ie ei ie ei ie ei ie ei ie ei ie ei

Check up on *ie* and *ei*

The following words are missing from "Fierce Justice": *society, reprieve, chief, brief, feigned, achievement, lenient.* Can you choose the right one to replace each numbered gap? Next, see if you can rearrange the jumbled words in "Tips for Tops" to find Dr Ivor Cure's hints for a healthy life.

Finally, *ie* and *ei* have been left out of the horoscopes below. But which combination completes each word?

Fierce Justice!

BANK ROBBER SENTENCED TO 125 YEARS

A judge has sentenced two men accused of robbing a bank at gunpoint to 125 years in prison. Throughout their ..1.. trial the men ..2.. innocence, in the hope of a ..3.. But the judge said he could not be ..4.. as the pair were obviously a menace to ..5.. . ..6.. Inspector Lawless said that putting these bad criminals behind bars was a great ..7.. .

TIPS FOR TOPS

1. Make sure your **tide** contains plenty of **tirpone**.
2. Watch your **thewig**.
3. Reduce your cholesterol intake - it's bad for your **seniv**.
4. Drink **dacefatfendie** coffee.
5. Eat a **yearvit** of foods, to make sure you get all the **sunnitret** necessary for good health.
6. Spend some of your **reelius** time each week exercising.
7. Meditate regularly, in order to **reeveil** stress and **texyain**.
8. Make sure you have a bath or shower every day. Personal **heegyin** is very important.

Star spot

Aquarius
You will rec..1..ve a gift.

Pisces
Don't get too t..2..d up with people's problems.

Aries
Have a night out with fr..3..nds.

Taurus
Watch out for counterf..4..t money.

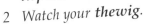
Gemini
The results of a sc..5..ntific experiment will interest you.

Cancer
You will take ..6..ther a boat or plane trip.

Leo
Make a recipe using unusual ingred..7..nts.

Virgo
Don't let a stranger dec..8..ve you.

Libra
S..9..ze the chance for a new exper..10..nce.

Scorpio
It's a good time to begin learning a for..11..gn language.

Sagittarius
Visit some anc..12..nt ruins.

Capricorn
You will hear from a distant relation, perhaps a nephew or n..13..ce.

23

Words with double letters (such as nece*ss*ary) are confusing to spell. But knowing whether to double a final letter when adding a suffix is even more tricky. It depends on the number of syllables in a word and where the stress lies. There are also special rules for words ending in *r* and *l*.

one When adding a suffix to a word of one syllable, a short vowel sound and one final consonant* (such as *glad*), double the final letter if the suffix begins with a vowel (*glad* + *en* = *gladden*). But leave the final letter single if the suffix begins with a consonant (*glad* + *ly* = *gladly*).

l Double a final *l* if the suffix begins with a vowel (*travel* + *ed* + *travelled*). But keep the *l* single if the suffix begins with a consonant (*quarrel* + *some* = *quarrelsome*), or if there are two vowels before it (*veil* + *ed* = *veiled*, *appeal* + *ing* = *appealing*). There are some exceptions, such as *formality*, *brutality*, *civility*, *capital/capitalism*, *fatal/fatalist/fatalism*.

r A final *r* stays single if the stress is on the first syllable (for example, *offer/offering*). If the stress is on the second syllable, double the *r* (for example, *occur/occurring*). But if there are two vowels before the *r*, leave it single (as in *despair/despairing*).

two For two-syllable words which end in one consonant* (such as *pilot*), don't double the final letter if the stress falls on the first syllable (for example, *pilot* + *ing* = *piloting*, *gallop* + *ed* = *galloped*). When the stress lies on the second syllable, double the final letter if the suffix begins with a vowel, but leave it single if it begins with a consonant. For example, *regret* + *ing* = *regretting*, but *regret* + *fully* = *regretfully*.

Missing doubles

Double *b, c, d, f, g, l, m, n, p, r, s, t* and *z* are missing from the pages of this story. But which do you need to complete each word?

I had had a fu..1..y feeling about things from the begi..2..ing. I had mi..3..ed my co..4..ection - the last train till morning, so asked someone (a sma..5.. man with a shifty a..6..earance and a nervous ma..7..er) to reco..8..end a hotel. Leaving my lu..9..age, I set off. The weather was ho..10..ible - to..11..ential rain poured down my co..12..ar and co..13..ected in my boots, while the wind whi..14..ed around me. After walking for ages down a deserted road, with no sign of any a..15..o..16..dation, I was ge..17..ing i..18..itable and depre..19..ed. Su..20..enly, I saw da..21..ling headlights coming from the o..22..osite direction. I a..23..empted to a..24..ract the driver's a..25..ention, but the car a..26..elerated as it a..27..roached! I leapt out of the way, just avoiding a co..28..ision, and ho..29..led to the side of the road. Having na..30..owly avoided a te..31..ible a..32..ident, I was also u..33..erly lost. What was I to do? Just then, I noticed a light in the distance. I trudged towards it through the su..34..ounding darkne..35.., over pe..36..les and through pu..37..les of mu..38..y water, until eventua..39..y

I a..40..ived at a sha..41..y li..42..le co..43..age.
    I knocked, cautiously, but there was no reply. Su..44..re..45..ing my nerves, I heaved the door open with a great e..46..ort, and ste..47..ed into a dark pa..48..age. On my i..49..ediate right stairs led down - I a..50..ume to the ce..51..ar. An o..52..ensive sme..53.. came wafting up. In a room to my left, a table was set with food and a cup of co..54..ee - still warm. I was pu..55..led as to why the o..56..upant had left in such a hu..57..y. But before I could satisfy my a..58..etite by a..59..acking the food, I realized with a shu..60..er that I was not alone! I turned around to find myself looking down the ba..61..el of a gun. A man with a ha..62..ard expre..63..ion was calmly si..64..ing by the door, behind me. I hoped he didn't have an itchy tri..65..er finger. I could tell he was a profe..66..ional vi..67..ain by the way he said, "Don't make it nece..68..ary for me to shoot you." I didn't like his a..69..itude one bit. But as my mo..70..o is "never say die," I determined to try to escape at the first o..71..ortunity, or find a way to get a me..72..age to someone, somehow.

*When a word ends with two consonants, the final letter always stays single. For example, *start* + *ed* = *started*, *prevent* + *ing* = *preventing*.

Watch out for the double letters in these words:

ACCURATE
VACCINATE
PROFESSION
IRRITATE
DESICCATE
SUGGEST
POSSESS
AGGRESSION
EMBARRASS
ADDRESS
INFLAMMABLE
DISSECT
APPLAUSE
ACCURATE
CORRESPOND
NECESSARY
ERROR
ASSESS
COMMAND
QUESTIONNAIRE
COMMUNICATION
EXAGGERATE
INTERRUPT
DISAPPOINT
ECCENTRIC
INTERROGATE
SUCCEED
PARALLEL

Doubling decisions

Here is an interview with Bob Barley, singer with The Howlers. To make it read correctly, try adding an ending to each word in capitals. But watch out for any letters that need doubling.

Q How did you become a star?
A I can DIM remember asking for a guitar when I was three. I SHOW that I was REAL talented as soon as I START playing.

Q Have you had any setbacks?
A In the BEGIN things moved SLOW and I had HARD any money. But FAIL never CROSS my mind. I GRAB the chance of RECORD my first single, "I'm FALL for you babe", and I never LOOK back.

Q What do you like best about your job?
A TRAVEL the world and SING live. HEAR the crowd CHEER at the OPEN of a concert is the GREAT FEEL in the world, man.

Q How do you like to spend Sunday?
A STAY in bed and FLIP through the newspapers while SIP a cup of tea.

Q What's the worst aspect of being famous?
A Being SPOT by fans and MOB wherever I go.

Q Do you ever think of QUIT the business?
A As I get OLD, I do think about STEP down and LET the youngsters take over. But although my hair's GET THIN, I'm not giving up yet.

Q When can we expect a new album from The Howlers?
A We've just SCRAP our latest material to try a change of direction. We're JAM in the studio at the moment.

Q What's your DEEP fear?
A DROP out of the charts and my fans FORGET me.

Q What are your REMAIN aims?
A I want to be an even BIG star!

Problem patterns

Here are some tricky spelling patterns. Look at the base word, then decide whether the missing consonants should be single or double in the words which follow.

1	panel	pane_ed pane_ing pane_ist	7	common	commo_er commo_est commo_ess
2	enrol	enro_ment enro_ed enro_ing	8	quarrel	quarre_some quarre_ing quarre_ed
3	open	ope_er ope_ing ope_ess	9	forget	forge_able forge_ing forge_ful
4	model	mode_ed mode_ing	10	commit	commi_ee commi_ing commi_ment
5	occasion	occasio_al occasio_ally	11	occur	occu_ed occu_ing occu_ence
6	label	labe_ed labe_ing			

12	cruel	crue_er crue_est crue_y crue_ty
13	star	sta_dom sta_ed sta_ing
14	commission	commissio_er commissio_ing
15	equal	equa_ize equa_ity equa_ed equa_ing
16	happen	happe_ing happe_ed

Here are some especially difficult tests. If you can answer all these correctly, you can be sure that you are an excellent speller!

c or s?

A few words are spelled with *c* when they are nouns, but with *s* when verbs. For example, *advice* and *advise*, *device* and *devise*, *prophecy* and *prophesy*. The pronunciation of these words changes with the spelling, but *practice* and *practise*, and *licence* and *license* sound the same spelled either way.

there/there's/their/theirs/they're

These spellings are very often confused. *There* is the opposite of *here*. *Their* and *theirs* show ownership (for example, *their books*, and *the books are theirs*). *They're* is short for *they are*. *There's* can mean two things: it is usually short for *there is*, but when followed by *been*, it is a short form of *there has*.

Homophones

Homophones are words which sound the same, but which have different spellings and meanings. For example, *there*, *their* and *they're*; *no* and *know*; *past* and *passed*; *threw* and *through*.

Watch out for words which have an "f" sound spelled *ph*. Here are some for you to test yourself on.

PHASE
ORPHAN
PHOBIA
GRAPH
CENOTAPH
PHYSIQUE
EPITAPH
SPHERE
ELEPHANT
PHONOGRAM
PHANTOM
NEPHEW
MICROPHONE
NYMPH
PHRASE
PARAGRAPH
PHEASANT
PHLEGM
CATASTROPHE
METAPHOR
PAMPHLET
PARAPHERNALIA
APOSTROPHE
PHARMACY
PHENOMENON
PHYSIOTHERAPY
DIAPHRAGM

Can you do better?

Here is Ike Canspellit's school report. His teachers have made a lot of spelling mistakes - can you spot them all?

Subject	Name *Ike Canspellit* Class *Upper 4* Comments	Grade
SPORT	Ike is skillfull on the football feeld and in the swiming pool.	B+
MUSIC	More self-disiplin and practise are neccesary, but Ike has a good scents of rithum.	C
DRAMA	IKE INJOYS BOTH TRADGEDY AND COMIDY AND IS A TALENTED CARACTER ACTER.	B
MATHS	Ike has benifitted from atending extra classes. He has definitely improoved, but still makes fawlts threw carelesness	C+
JOGRAPHY	Ike's prodject on equitorial rain forrest's was very nollidgible.	B-
SCIENCE	Ike is unintrested in sience and looses consentration easily. He also displays a tendancy to talk. During practicle work in the laboratory he medals with the eeqipment. His techneeks are very disapointing.	D
HISTRY	Ike has a thurugh under standing of the Ainshent World, espeshally of the lifes of the Roman emperors. He has enjoyed lerning about the gods and godeses of Greek mitholojee.	A-
INGLISH	Altho Ike makes littel errers in his grammer, his creativ riting is genrally exsellent. His discriptions are perseptive and ofen humorus. We have been greatful for his asistence in the libry this year. As usuall, Ike is top of the class at spelling.	A+

Signature *Ms V. Unfriendly* Date *July 1st*

Noun or verb?

Each of these sentences has two words with either *c* or *s* missing. Can you spell them correctly?

1   My piano teacher says that practi_e makes perfect - but I hate practi_ing!
2   A clairvoyant prophe_ied my future, but I will be surprised if her prophe_y comes true.
3   An inventor has devi_ed a new devi_e to wake you up in the morning.
4   Everyone should buy a dog licen_e in order to licen_e their dog.
5   I advi_ed him not to give up, but he took no notice of my good advi_e.

Sound-alike

Can you pick the correct spellings from the homophones on this page of Wendy's diary?

5th April

The weather/whether today was fowl/foul, but I'd promised to meat/meet Grandad at half passed/past two/to/too. He was already/all ready there. He waived/waved when he saw/sore me. He said he'd only had a short wait/weight. He asked if I'd mist/missed him - of course/coarse! It was poring/pouring with rain, but we wandered/wondered along the beach/beech anyway. He said I'd groan/grown since he'd last scene/seen me - what a complement/compliment! I said he should try dyeing/dying his white hair/hare. He laughed, and tolled/told me that he hated the whole/hole business of

Saturday

getting old. He said it seemed only yesterday when he used to read bedtime stories/storeys aloud/allowed to me. We talked about how board/bored I am at school. Grandad said I should no/know that every lessen/lesson is important, and that my opinion will alter/altar. That maybe/may be sow/so/sew, but I'm shore/sure I'll never enjoy chemistry! I led/lead the way to the station to ensure/insure that he didn't get lost. He asked me to right/write soon, and gave me some stationery/stationary with my name and address at the top of every peace/piece of paper.

Can you get *there*?

Can you think of shorter ways to say the underlined parts of these sentences?

You will have to use *there*, *there's*, *their*, *theirs*, or *they're* in each one.

1   Look! <u>There is</u> Michelle!
2   Look at that, over <u>in that direction</u>!
3   I know <u>they are</u> going away today.
4   <u>The house belonging to them</u> is huge.
5   I want one just like <u>the one they have</u>.
6   <u>There has</u> been a dreadful accident.
7   Drop it! It's <u>the one belonging to them</u>.
8   <u>There has</u> been a snowfall overnight.
9   I liked <u>the friends belonging to them</u>.
10 Have some more. <u>There is</u> plenty left.
11 I hate going <u>to that place</u>.
12 <u>They are</u> always arguing.

The final frontier

Here are just a few of the most commonly misspelled words. Why not make your own list of difficult spellings?

ACCOMMODATION
ACKNOWLEDGE
AERIAL
ALCOHOL
ALTOGETHER
AMATEUR
ANNIHILATE
APARTMENT
AWKWARD

BACHELOR
BANKRUPTCY
BEAUTIFUL
BUSINESS

CALIBRE
CALENDAR
CAMOUFLAGE
CARICATURE
CEMETERY
COLONEL
CONSCIOUS
CRITICISM

DECREPIT
DESCENDANT
DISSUADE

ENVIRONMENT
EXERCISE
EXHAUST

FLUORESCENT
FOREIGNER

GASES
GAUGE
GUARANTEE

IDYLLIC
INDISPENSABLE
INSTALMENT

LIAISON
LIQUEFIED

MEDIEVAL
OCCASION
OPPORTUNITY

PECULIAR
PERSEVERANCE
POSSESSION
PREJUDICE
PURSUE
PRIVILEGE

QUESTIONNAIRE

RECOMMEND
RHYME

SECRETARY
SEPARATE
SILHOUETTE
SURPRISE

VACUUM
VEHICLE
VICIOUS

27

Page 3

What are syllables?

one syllable: soap, bread, milk, eggs, cheese
two syllables: tooth/paste, pea/nuts, coff/ee, hon/ey, on/ions
three syllables: det/er/gent, lem/on/ade, tom/a/toes, ba/na/nas, or/an/ges
four syllables: mac/a/ro/ni, cau/li/flow/er

What is stress?

tooth/paste, _pea_/nuts, _hon_/ey, _coff_/ee, _on_/ions, det/_er_/gent, lem/on/_ade_, tom/_a_/toes, ba/_na_/nas, _or_/an/ges, mac/a/_ro_/ni, _cau_/li/flow/er

Pages 4-5

An eye for an _i_

1 bikini 3 confetti 5 taxi 7 ski 9 khaki
2 safari 4 graffiti 6 spaghetti 8 mini 10 salami

Double trouble

What beautiful weather!

I heard it'll cloud over and rain later today.

People confuse us because we're so alike.

Your bargain blue jeans really suit you.

I've been waiting an hour for my friend.

I said we'd leave at the usual time.

Please can we look around again first?

One vowel short

1 _o_ is the missing vowel 4 _y_ is the missing vowel
2 _u_ is the missing vowel 5 _i_ is the missing vowel
3 _a_ is the missing vowel 6 _e_ is the missing vowel

Silent _e_

1 The new words are:
us, not, fat, spit, mad, hop, rat, kit, cut, rip
These all have short vowel sounds.

2 The new words are:
bare, rage, huge, care, fire, sage, fare, pare, wage, here

3 The completed words are:
Chinese, shape, white, telephone, confuse, alone, produce, alive, suppose, complete, escape, home, rescue, combine, bathe, appetite, celebrate, amuse, severe, supreme
These vowels all have long sounds because of the silent e on the end of each word.

Pages 6-7

Sp_ies_ in the sk_ies_

the _ys_ organization:
convoys, essays, toys, holidays, valleys, keys, displays, delays, trolleys, abbeys, journeys

the _ies_ organization:
activities, bullies, enemies, allies, flies, factories, dictionaries, replies, bodies, parties, cherries, opportunities, centuries, galaxies

O! What now?

Eskimo/Eskimo**s** mosquito/mosquito**es**
igloo/igloo**s** piano/piano**s**
kangaroo/kangaroo**s** potato/potato**es**
buffalo/buffalo**es** tomato/tomato**es**
volcano/volcano**es** photo/photo**s**

Singularly confused

1 termini 4 gateaux 6 formulae
2 fungi 5 syllabi or 7 crises
3 larvae syllabuses 8 media

_F_ words

1 puff**s** 6 thie**ves**, safe**s**
2 scarf**s** or scar**ves**, 7 li**ves**
handkerchief**s**, 8 shel**ves**, loa**ves**
yoursel**ves** 9 wol**ves**
3 hoof**s** or hoo**ves** 10 wi**ves**
4 lea**ves** 11 roof**s**
5 hal**ves**

Plural puzzler

Irregular plurals include:
mice, men, women, geese, children, teeth, feet

Words that are the same in both the singular and the plural include:
deer, salmon, trout, grouse, moose, news, fish, mathematics, series, species, innings

Pages 8-9

Er...? Uh...?

THINGS TO BUY:
pizza, sugar, butter, flour, tuna, bananas, hamburgers, marmalade, chocolate flavour milkshake, writing paper and envelopes, an eraser, a ruler and a pair of scissors,
2 metres of purple ribbon, film for my camera, a packet of cake mixture, a battery for my calculator, a birthday present for Samantha

Remember to take my purse!

THINGS TO DO:
1 Cut out some pictures of famous actors for my project.
2 Sign up for the class trip to the theatre.
3 Ask my next-door neighbour if I can look for my basketball in his garden.
4 See if my sister will let me wear her new dress on Saturday.
5 Remind Amanda that it's our turn this week to look after the earthworms in the science room. (Yuk!)

Conquer kicking *k*

Kevin likes:
sna**k**es and **cro**codiles
hearing his voice e**ch**o
pi**cn**i**ck**ing in the par**k**
boo**k**s about shipwre**ck**s
doing magi**c** tri**ck**s
climbing trees

Kevin dislikes:
a**c**ting in s**ch**ool plays
singing in the **ch**oir
losing his train ti**ck**et
stoma**ch** a**ch**e
cornflakes, **ch**i**ck**en
and bro**cc**oli
chemistry lessons

Are you an *air*-head?

Dear Gran

My first time on an aeroplane was really exciting - when I'm a millionaire I'm going to have my own private jet. My suitcase was bulging - Dad says I'll never have time to wear all the clothes and pairs of shoes I've brought. But I still managed to forget my hair brush, and Sue's forgotten her teddy bear.
   We've got a lovely room to share that looks out on the sea - there are some rare birds to spot along this part of the coast. We're going to a funfair tomorrow.
   Take care - we'll see you soon,
      Love
      Donna XXXXXXXX

Be sure of *sh*, *shun* and *zhun*

1 colli**sion**
2 electri**cian**
3 investiga**tion**
4 explo**sion**
5 junc**tion**
6 confu**sion**
7 ca**sh**
8 anxious
9 informa**tion**
10 i**ss**ued
11 descrip**tion**
12 suspi**cion**
13 mousta**che**
14 offi**cial**
15 expre**ssion**
16 ini**tials**
17 **ch**auffeur

══════ Pages 10-11 ══════

Tongue twister teasers

1 h   2 g   3 l   4 k   5 b   6 h   7 w   8 n   9 h

Conversation clues

1 **wh**at
2 **p**alm
3 **p**sychic
4 a**gh**ast
5 **k**new
6 campai**gn**
7 lam**b**
8 yol**k**
9 ra**sp**berries
10 **k**new
11 desi**gn**er
12 exhi**b**ition
13 **sh**ould
14 s**c**issors
15 **w**ould
16/17 ya**ch**t
18 forei**gn**
19 i**s**lands
20 han**d**some
21/22 ri**gh**t

Hear this

1 vege**t**able
2 Febr**u**ary
3 mini**a**ture
4 valu**a**ble
5 twel**f**th
6 choco**l**ate
7 tempe**r**ature
8 parli**a**ment
9 vac**uu**m
10 extra**o**rdinary
11 gene**r**al
12 dia**m**ond
13 monas**t**ery
14 We**d**nesday

The sound of silence

1 bom**b**
2 cu**p**board
3 din**gh**y
4 **w**restler
5 **k**nocker
6 recei**p**t
7 crum**b**s
8 b**u**oy
9 **k**nife
10 cas**t**le

══════ Pages 12-13 ══════

Qu quiz

1 fre**qu**ent
2 opa**que**
3 s**qu**irrel
4 **qu**it
5 tran**qu**il
6 a**qu**arium
7 **qu**arter
8 **qu**arry
9 uni**que**
10 s**qu**are
11 **qu**ick
12 con**qu**eror
13 **qu**ay
14 **qu**antity
15 s**qu**ander

16 a**qu**educt
17 **qu**arrel
18 **qu**artet
19 **qu**eer
20 **qu**een

ge or *dge*?

1 colle**ge**
2 stran**ge**
3 emer**ged**
4 he**dge**hog
5 ba**dger**
6 ca**ge**
7 ju**dge**
8 crin**ged**
9 Mi**dget**
10 mana**ged**
11 le**dge**
12 fi**dget**
13 he**dge**hog
14 dama**ge**
15 ima**ge**
16 exchan**ged**
17 Smu**dge**
18 ba**dge**

Choose *ch* or *tch*

1 Kit**ch**en
2 Pun**ch**-up
3 sandwi**ch**es
4 lun**ch**
5 Fren**ch**
6 Dut**ch**
7 scor**ch**ing
8 **ch**icken
9 swit**ch**ing
10 tou**ch**ed
11 ma**tch**
12 wat**ch**ed
13 **ch**eered
14 **ch**ased
15 clu**tch**ing
16 bu**tch**er's
17 ha**tch**et
18 ba**tch**
19 ket**ch**up
20 pun**ch**ed
21 ben**ch**
22 pi**tch**ed
23 wren**ch**ing
24 stre**tch**er
25 fe**tch**ed
26 sti**tch**es
27 cru**tch**es

the *gh* trap

══════ Pages 14-15 ══════

Guesswork

trans	across/beyond	**auto**	self
re	again	**multi**	many/much
hyper	too much	**photo**	light
post	after	**anti**	against/opposing
micro	very small	**pre**	before
circum	around	**extra**	beyond/outside
omni	all	**mono**	single

Singled out

1 antenatal - before birth
2 ultramodern - extremely modern
3 pseudonym - a false name, such as used by an author
4 demigod - a half-human, half-immortal being
5 homophones - words which sound the same
6 intravenous - within a vein
7 megastar - a very famous personality
8 hypothermia - abnormally low body temperature
9 archbishop - chief bishop

29

Pages 14-15 continued

Picture this

1	centi	3	semi	5	un	7	hemi	9	tri
2	tele	4	super	6	bi	8	inter	10	sub

Matching pairs

1	subzero	6	dishonest	11	surmount
2	interchange	7	illegal	12	precaution
3	underground	8	upstairs	13	biannual
4	misconduct	9	irresponsible	14	innumerable
5	extraordinary	10	return		

Precise prefixes

1	multicoloured	6	underdone	11	anticlimax
2	postpone	7	disappear	12	dissatisfied
3	autobiography	8	decode	13	monotone
4	bilingual	9	always	14	transform
5	preview	10	research	15	imperfect

Face the opposition

disobey, unnecessary, illegible, irreplaceable, independent, improbable, illegal, miscalculations, disapproved, impossible, impatiently, irresponsible, misfortune, irreversible, dissimilar, unmanageable, indecisive, impolite

Pages 16-17

Get guessing

Did you **guess** it was me?
I'm so good at **disguising** myself that even my **colleagues** don't recognize me. I **guarantee** I'll solve any mystery, however **intriguing** it is. If you know where to look, you can always find clues to **guide** you to a **guilty** person.
At the moment, I'm undercover as a musician - that's why I've got a **guitar**. But unluckily musical notes are a foreign **language** to me. I have to be on my **guard** all the time so I don't blow my cover.
Shhhh! Someone's coming.
I'd better **get** away...

Putting an end to it

1	peaceable or peaceful	9	glanced
2	slicing	10	charging
3	spacious	11	judgement or judgment
4	unmanageable	12	scarcely
5	outrageously	13	dancing
6	spicy	14	courageous
7	noticeable	15	balancing
8	juicy	16	advantageous

Do you get the gist?

1	geography	7	margin	13	bandage
2	giraffe	8	origin	14	savage
3	image	9	apology	15	genius
4	germs	10	oxygen	16	cage
5	dingy	11	stingy		
6	garage	12	giant		

Spell soft *c*

1 Crunch-U-Like. Try our new **cereal**!
We guarantee you'll love our **recipe** of crunchy oats and **juicy citrus** fruit chunks or your money back.

2 Merriman's **Circus** opens at 8pm with a **magnificent procession**.
Gaze at the **precision** of knife-throwers, the **concentration** of jugglers, the **grace** of trapeze artists, the **balance** of high-wire walkers.
Gasp in **excitement** as Stevie Star spins two hundred **saucers** and Marvin the Marvellous **unicyclist** makes a steep **ascent** up a tightrope.
Laugh at the **excellent** clowns!
Be **deceived** by the world-famous magician "the Great Mysterio".
See the greatest show of the **century**.

3 Sample the **peace** of Writington Nature Reserve.
A brief film-show in our mini-**cinema introduces** the many different **species** you can see.
Wander around our **circular** nature trail at your own **convenience**.
Don't forget to visit the swannery where you can watch **cygnets** and parent swans in their natural habitat.
Why not stop for refreshment at our self-**service** café? See you soon!

Pages 18-19

wise or *wize*?

1	recognized/ recognised	6	specializes/ specialises	10	advertised
2	exercise	7	hypnotize/ hypnotise	11	improvise
3	revised			12	despise
4	supervise	8	pressurized/ pressurised	13	criticizes/ criticises
5	organized/ organised, surprise	9	prize	14	disguised
				15	prise

Probably horrible

1	convert**ible**	8	horr**ible**	15	sens**ible**
2	vis**ible**	9	soci**able**	16	respons**ible**
3	recogniz**able**	10	peace**able**	17	gull**ible**
4	advis**able**	11	understand**able**		
5	unmov**able**	12	incred**ible**	18	poss**ible**
6	terr**ible**	13	unbeliev**able**	19	unforgett**able**
7	collaps**ible**	14	reli**able**		

Possibly problematical

1	physical	5	pickle	9	monocle
2	circle	6	critical	10	vehicle
3	obstacle	7	ankle	11	bicycle
4	icicle	8	classical	12	local

Trail finder

The letter *a* is missing from: acquaintance, clearance, allowance, ignorant, rampant, defendant, grievance, servant, important, instant, fragrant, reluctance, perseverance, appearance, disturbance, nuisance, appliance, assistant, observant, lieutenant, attendance, tenant, resemblance, insurance, ambulance. The letter *e* is missing from all the other words in the grid. The path looks like this:

Pages 20-21

How about *ous*?

1	glamorous	5	studious	9	rigorous
2	dangerous	6	anxious	10	cautious
3	mountainous	7	mischievous		
4	humorous	8	laborious		

Now you see it...

1	curiosity	7	forty	13	monstrous
2	hindrance	8	pronunciation	14	vanity
3	repetition	9	waitress	15	remembrance
4	exclamation	10	maintenance	16	ninth
5	disastrous	11	wintry		
6	administrate	12	explanation		

All's well that ends well

writing, celebration, amusement, renovation, exciting, amazing, scary, extremely, daring, revolving, imagine, adventurous, driving, argument, useless, persuading, tiring, noisy, behaviour, sensibly, coming, hoping, truly, invitations, likely, nervous, ridiculous

What to do with *y*

worry + ing = worrying
destroy + er = destroyer
hurry + ed = hurried
employ + ment = employment
mystery + ous = mysterious
happy + ness = happiness

sly + ly = slyly
tidy + er = tidier
lazy + ly = lazily
crazy + est = craziest
dry + ly = drily
glory + ous = glorious

Other possible combinations are: worrier, worried, destroying, destroyed, hurrying, hurriedly, employer, employing, employed, mysteriously, happier, happily, happiest, tidily, tidying, tidiest, tidied, tidiness, slyest, slyness, crazier, crazily, craziness, crazied, lazier, laziest, laziness, glorying, gloried, drying, dried, drier, driest, dryness

Pages 22-23

i and *e* quick quiz

1	thief	4	field	7	shield
2	eight	5	tie	8	soldier
3	view	6	handkerchief		

Missing p*ie*ces

1	neighbours	4	disobedient	7	unveiled
2	patience priest	5	pieces of eight	8	heir
3	Eiffel	6	sleigh, reindeer		

Fierce Justice

1	brief	4	lenient	7	achievement
2	feigned	5	society		
3	reprieve	6	chief		

Tips for Tops

1	diet, protein	4	decaffeinated	7	relieve, anxiety
2	weight	5	variety, nutrients	8	hygiene
3	veins	6	leisure		

Star Spot

1	receive	6	either	11	foreign
2	tied	7	ingredients	12	ancient
3	friends	8	deceive	13	niece
4	counterfeit	9	seize		
5	scientific	10	experience		

Pages 24-25

Missing doubles

1	funny	5	small	9	luggage
2	beginning	6	appearance	10	horrible
3	missed	7	manner	11	torrential
4	connection	8	recommend	12	collar

31

Pages 24-25 continued

13 collected
14 whipped
15/16 accommodation
17 getting
18 irritable
19 depressed
20 suddenly
21 dazzling
22 opposite
23 attempted
24 attract
25 attention
26 accelerated
27 approached
28 collision
29 hobbled
30 narrowly
31 terrible
32 accident
33 utterly
34 surrounding
35 darkness
36 pebbles
37 puddles
38 muddy
39 eventually
40 arrived
41 shabby
42 little
43 cottage
44/45 suppressing
46 effort
47 stepped
48 passage
49 immediate
50 assume
51 cellar
52 offensive
53 smell
54 coffee
55 puzzled
56 occupant
57 hurry
58 appetite
59 attacking
60 shudder
61 barrel
62 haggard
63 expression
64 sitting
65 trigger
66 professional
67 villain
68 necessary
69 attitude
70 motto
71 opportunity
72 message

Doubling decisions

dimly, showed, really, started, beginning, slowly, hardly, failure/failing, crossed, grabbed, recording, falling, looked, travelling, singing, hearing, cheering, opening, greatest, feeling, staying, flipping, sipping, spotted, mobbed, quitting, older, stepping, letting, getting, thinner, scrapped, jamming, deepest, dropping, forgetting, remaining, bigger

Problem patterns

1	panelled	panelling	panellist
2	enrolment	enrolled	enrolling
3	opener	opening	openness
4	modelled	modelling	
5	occasional	occasionally	
6	labelled	labelling	
7	commoner	commonest	commonness
8	quarrelsome	quarrelling	quarrelled
9	forgettable	forgetting	forgetful
10	committee	committing	commitment
11	occurred	occurring	occurrence
12	crueller cruelty	cruellest	cruelly
13	stardom	starred	starring
14	commissioner	commissioning	
15	equalize equalling	equality	equalled
16	happening	happened	

Pages 26-27

Noun or verb?

1 My piano teacher says that practice makes perfect - but I hate practising!
2 A clairvoyant prophesied my future, but I will be surprised if her prophecy comes true.
3 An inventor has devised a new device to wake you up in the morning.
4 Everyone should buy a dog licence in order to license their dog.
5 I advised him not to give up, but he took no notice of my good advice.

Sound-alike

weather, foul, meet, past, two, already, waved, saw, wait, missed, course, pouring, wandered, beach, grown, seen, compliment, dyeing, hair, told, whole, stories, aloud, bored, know, lesson, alter, may be, so, sure, led, ensure, write, stationery, piece

Can you do better?

SPORT   Ike is skilful on the football field and in the swimming pool.

MUSIC   More self-discipline and practice are necessary, but Ike has a good sense of rhythm.

DRAMA   IKE ENJOYS BOTH TRAGEDY AND COMEDY AND IS A TALENTED CHARACTER ACTOR.

MATHS   Ike has benefited from attending extra classes. He has definitely improved, but still makes faults through carelessness.

GEOGRAPHY   Ike's project on equatorial rain forests was very knowledgeable.

SCIENCE   Ike is uninterested in science and loses concentration easily. He also displays a tendency to talk. During practical work in the laboratory he meddles with the equipment. His techniques are very disappointing.

HISTORY   Ike has a thorough understanding of the Ancient World, especially of the lives of the Roman emperors. He has enjoyed learning about the gods and goddesses of Greek mythology.

ENGLISH   Although Ike makes little errors in his grammar, his creative writing is generally excellent. His descriptions are perceptive and often humorous. We have been grateful for his assistance in the library this year. As usual, Ike is top of the class at spelling.

Can you get there?

1 Look! **There's** Michelle!
2 Look at that, over **there**!
3 I know **they're** going away today.
4 **Their** house is huge.
5 I want one just like **theirs**
6 **There's** been a dreadful accident.
7 Drop it! It's **theirs**.
8 **There's** been a snowfall overnight.
9 I liked **their** friends.
10 Have some more. **There's** plenty left.
11 I hate going **there**.
12 **They're** always arguing.

PUNCTUATION

CONTENTS

When you are writing, do you ever wonder if you need a comma (,) or an apostrophe ('), and where to put them? If so, you can find out more in this section. These marks are part of punctuation. If you do all the puzzles in this section of the book, good punctuation will become second nature. On the way, clear rules and tips will help you learn how to use each mark.

What is punctuation for?

Punctuation is a set of marks that you use in writing to divide up groups of words and make them easier to read.

When speaking, you vary the speed and loudness of words. In writing, punctuation shows these variations. It helps make the meaning clear because it shows how you would say the words, as well as where sentences begin, slow down and end.

See how the meaning changes depending on the punctuation you use:

Sam and Lucy, don't eat all that junk food!

Sam and Lucy don't eat all that junk food.

Without punctuation, even words that can only have one meaning are hard to read. Compare these letters, for instance:

dear mrs peters
my dog lucky has disappeared i think i heard him barking inside your garage so i think he has got stuck in there i would really appreciate your help in finding my dog please ring me or my dad when you get home
    tina

Dear Mrs Peters,
My dog Lucky has disappeared. I think I heard him barking inside your garage, so I think he has got stuck in there.
I would really appreciate your help in finding my dog. Please ring me or my Dad when you get home.
    Tina

Punctuation is a vital writing skill. You need this skill to ensure that your writing is clear. It is also essential if you want to write more than very basic English.

Using this part of the book

This section looks at each punctuation mark in turn. Read through the guidelines, then test your punctuation skills by trying the puzzles which follow.

The book is not designed for writing in, so have some paper and a pen ready for your answers. You can check these at the back of the section.

Don't worry if you make mistakes. Work through the puzzles, then go back to anything you found hard.

You will come across a few grammatical terms, such as *subject, verb* etc. You can use the index on page 96 to find out where each term is explained.

How much punctuation?

SAM!!!!

In cartoon strips, you sometimes see lots of punctuation. This is because there is not enough room to explain the atmosphere and the characters' feelings. Extra punctuation is used instead.

Avoid using this much. Use enough for your meaning to be clear and no more. To show that someone said something in a particular way, describe how they said it, instead of relying on punctuation. For example: *"Sam!" he called angrily.*

The book explains the rules you should follow. In formal writing, such as essays and letters to people you don't know well, keep close to the rules. In other situations, you can be more flexible. If you are unsure, write short sentences. They are much easier to punctuate than long ones.

Punctuation summary

This shows you the different punctuation marks, each with its name and an example in which it is used. You will find out all about them as you work through this section of the book. Check that you can recognize them all, then do the puzzle below.

.	full stop	**They have seen some shirts they want.**	
,	comma	**I like chicken, sausages and chocolate.**	
:	colon	**Here's what you must bring: a swimsuit, a towel and a sandwich.**	
;	semicolon	**The view is fine; the broken window is the problem.**	
?	question mark	**Who is that?**	
!	exclamation mark	**That video is so stupid!**	
'	apostrophe	**Sarah's hat**	
" "	quotation marks	**He said, "Please wait for us by the fountain."**	
( )	brackets	**Win a luxury holiday for two (details next week).**	
-	hyphen	**I am a little short-sighted.**	
–	dash	**It is not a problem – just inconvenient.**	
A B C	capital letters	**At first, we found King Pong scary.**	

Testing correspondence

How many of each of the following are there in this letter: full stops, commas, colons, semicolons, exclamation marks, hyphens, quotation marks, question marks and apostrophes?

The Select Residential College
Blimpton-on-Sea
3 September 1995

Dear Mr and Mrs Fishplaite,
It is my sad duty to write to you regarding your daughter, Sonia, whom we must ask you to withdraw from S.R.C.
Sonia's attitude and manners have dramatically deteriorated; the poor quality of her work does nothing to compensate for this.
The events which prompted the decision are as follows: she locked her French teacher, Mademoiselle Ragou, in a cupboard and called her "an unenlightened stick-insect". She later called me "a Komodo dragon" in front of all the girls and my staff at morning assembly!
We will of course help you in any way possible, and Sonia can remain here until the end of term. Would you like us to obtain a place for her at Highwall College, an establishment with the strong, disciplinarian approach which your daughter needs?
I look forward to hearing from you in the very near future.
Yours sincerely,
K.D. Brittledge
Katrina Diana Brittledge
Headmistress

The full stop is the dot which you normally find at the end of a sentence. But it has several other uses too.

I just heard a cuckoo.

full stop

Ending a sentence

A sentence is a group of words that can stand on its own and make sense. It starts with a capital letter and must have a full stop at the end, unless you are using a question mark or an exclamation mark (see below).

A full stop at the end of a sentence stands for a clear pause. It shows where, if you were speaking, your voice would drop and you would stop for a moment.

Here are the only two cases in which you do not use a full stop to end a sentence:

1 If a sentence is a question, it must end with a question mark, not a full stop. For example: *Which gate number do I go to?* This is explained on page 44.

2 If a sentence is about a strong feeling, you can end it with an exclamation mark: *I hate that!* (See page 46.)

Sentence spotting

In order to know where to put full stops, you have to be able to spot a sentence.

To qualify as a sentence, a group of words must make sense when it stands on its own. A typical sentence has a subject (a person or thing doing the action) and a verb (an action word): *The postman opened the parcel.*

Sentences can be very short, though, and their meaning then depends on other sentences around them. Look at this example: *What did you say? Nothing.* Here, "nothing" is a sentence. If you know what was said before, it makes sense, and so it ends with a full stop.

Sentences can be linked with words like *and, but, so* or *because* to become one longer sentence, with a single full stop at the end. For example: *The postman opened the parcel and the counterfeit money fell out.*

Shortening words

You can put a full stop at the end of an abbreviation (a short form of a word), where it stands for the letters that you have not written out. For example:

	stands for
m.p.h.	miles per hour
U.N.	United Nations
J. Thomas	The initial, or first letter, J stands for the person's first name, John.

If an abbreviation is at the end of a sentence, use only one full stop: *She works for the U.N.*

The full stop after an abbreviation is optional. For example, both U.N. and UN are correct*. Use one whenever it helps to make your writing clear: for example, Mon. morning is clearer than Mon morning.

With words such as Mister that are shortened to their first and last letters, you do not use a full stop: for example, *Mr Thomas.*

Pen problems

This message has six full stops, but it also has black ink splodges that look like full stops. Copy it out, keeping only the six correct full stops.

I'll be home. late from school today, Mum. After volleyball practice, Miss. Mussly wants to discuss plans for our sports day. See you at about 6. p.m.. (Please. feed Misty as soon as you get in. Because of the kittens, I don't think. she should have to wait until 6.)

36

*For abbreviations which people read out as if they were words, such as UNESCO (which is said you-ness-coe), you normally do not use full stops.

Costly dots

Freddy is trying to write a message. He must add three full stops. Where should he put these to make his message as clear as possible?

> SORRY I LET YOU DOWN IN INVERNESS I'LL EXPLAIN WHEN I SEE YOU MY MONEY BELT WAS STILL IN YOUR BACKPACK WHEN YOU LEFT IN A HUFF PLEASE MEET ME FORT WILLIAM STATION ON SAT 8PM RIGHT OF LEFT-LUGGAGE LOCKERS.

Pointless

Five of these pieces of writing are sentences which should end with a full stop. Decide which they are, and then write them out, ending each one with a full stop**.

1   **Further up the coast, the explorer**
2   **In Japan, cats have no tails**
3   **They were**
4   **All of a sudden, it vanished**
5   **They suffered dreadfully from cold, hunger**
6   **He cannot go into**
7   **It all seemed highly**
8   **She grabbed the mobile phone, lurched forward and**
9   **Sam looked blank**
10 **In front of her**

Drifter's diary

This diary extract is written with no full stops at all. Write it out, adding as many full stops as possible and making sure that each sentence starts with a capital letter.

Monday

up at 11 am I didn't wash my sisters had left the bathroom in such a state that I didn't feel like it I went over to Jo Drone's Café for a hotdog because Dad was retiling the kitchen floor I just love that hot yellow mustard Teeny Tina came by for me later and we spent the whole afternoon at the DJ Club on my way home I bumped into my old classmate Sally Straite in Suburb Lane when I told her about how bored I felt, she told me to pull myself together and perhaps get a summer job she suggested I start by keeping a diary Sally thinks that the problems I have to iron out will soon become clear all I have to do is keep a diary for a few days and then read it through she reckons the problems will soon leap off the page at me

Sally's tel number is 666 3333 she said I can ring her whenever I need some moral support I'm going to clean up the bathroom now then I'm going to have a bath and go to bed it's 10 pm

Dotty dramas

The police are investigating a train robbery. They have received some information from an anonymous witness, but it is difficult to make sense of, as there is not much punctuation. Split it up into sentences, using full stops and capital letters.

I read the article in yesterday's Echo about the great pearl robbery I was on that train and am writing to let you know what I know there were hardly any passengers on the train in my carriage, there was only one man I noticed him because he had six briefcases and looked very nervous I soon dozed off all of a sudden, I woke up to the sound of terrible shouts a woman with a black mask over her face rushed towards me and threw a pile of prawn and mayonnaise sandwiches in my face and all over my clothes then she climbed out of the window onto the platform the woman disappeared into the night while I started trying to wipe off the

prawns and mayonnaise at this point, I discovered there were lots of blue pearls mixed in with the food I scraped as much as I could into a plastic bag and got off the train nobody noticed me go in all the commotion now that I have read about what happened to the man with the briefcases, I want to hand in the pearls you can phone me on 867 2382

**The hints on page 36 on how to spot a sentence will help you.

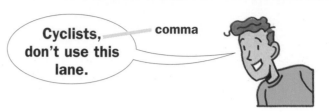

The comma stands for a short pause that separates a word or group of words from another in a sentence. You normally use it where you would pause very slightly if you were speaking. Commas are often essential to make the meaning clear.

Cyclists·don't use this lane has another meaning from the sentence above.

Commas in lists

When you list words in a sentence, use commas to separate them. Normally, if the last two parts of the list are joined with *and*, you don't put a comma in front of *and*. For example: *These are made from eggs, flour, water, cheese and herbs*.

Sometimes, though, you need a comma in front of *and*, to make sure the sentence is clear: *Jim ordered tomato soup, cheese, and coffee ice cream*. The comma makes clear that he did not order *cheese and coffee ice cream*!

When you list adjectives (describing words) before a noun (a naming word), commas between the adjectives are not always needed. In *deep, cold pond*, the comma sounds best. In *big blue eyes*, it is unnecessary. Put commas in when it would be natural to pause*.

Long sentences

To know where commas go in long sentences, it helps to know how sentences are made. A typical one has at least one main clause (this has a subject and a verb, makes sense on its own, and could itself be a sentence). It may also have 1) a subordinate clause – this too has a verb, but depends on a main clause for its meaning; 2) a phrase – this adds meaning; it is often short and says where, when or how something happens.

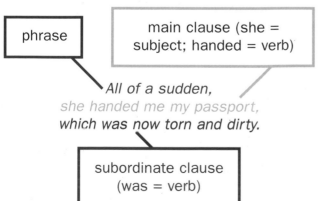

phrase

main clause (she = subject; handed = verb)

All of a sudden,
she handed me my passport,
which was now torn and dirty.

subordinate clause (was = verb)

Comma or no comma?

Here are some rules and guidelines on when to use commas in long sentences:
1 Put a comma in front of words like *but*, *although*, *so*, *yet* and *or* when you use them to link main clauses. For example: *It is a tough journey, so plan carefully***.

Leave out the comma when linking main clauses with *and*: *Our ship docked and the officers came aboard*. Put a comma in, though, if *and* introduces a new idea (*This is good news, and I shall pass it on*), or if it is needed for clarity.
2 Use a comma to separate off a phrase at the start of a sentence: *After this row, they felt better*. After a short phrase, the comma is optional.

If the phrase comes later, you may need commas on either side of it in order to make the meaning clear: *She whistled and luckily her dog followed* (commas are optional). *She whistled and, after a tiff with a passing cat, her dog followed* (commas here are best).
3 Commas may be needed to separate a subordinate clause from a main clause. If the subordinate clause is first, a comma is usual: *While Zoe wrote, Pip washed up*.
4 For a subordinate clause starting with *who*, *whom* or *which*, a comma must separate it off if it is not essential to the meaning. Leaving out the comma makes the clause a more important part of the sentence, and so may change its meaning. For example:

He threw away the eggs, which were broken.

He threw away the eggs which were broken.

*The comma can affect the meaning: compare *a pretty small girl* (quite small) with *a pretty, small girl* (pretty and small).
**In informal writing, people often leave out the comma when linking short main clauses: *It is tough so plan carefully*.

Two by two

For each pair of pictures below, there are two sentences. Match each sentence with the correct picture.

The apples, which were red, had worms in them.

The apples which were red had worms in them.

The boys, who were wearing red, all had black hair.

The boys who were wearing red all had black hair.

The ham, which was cold, came with salad.

The ham which was cold came with salad.

A comma or two

Copy out these sentences, adding one comma each to sentences 1 - 4, and two commas each to sentences 5 - 9.

1 My brother is lazy rude and arrogant.
2 Many people will read this story although it is very badly written.
3 Stefie has brought flowers ice cream and chocolates.
4 Meanwhile Susie was cycling home.
5 I took the books which were old torn and shabby but left the good ones for my mother.
6 The three bands that were playing were Sound and Emotion Billy and the Cheesemakers and the Blue Moon Band.
7 He waved at Lisa who was watching from the window and walked down the street.
8 The rugby players who were exhausted limped off the pitch together.

Lily's list

Lily has written out her shopping list without putting any commas in. Can you add 14 commas?

Chemist's:
new toothbrush aspirin and soap.
Butcher's:
sausages bacon and a leg of lamb.
Supermarket:
milk butter eggs flour sugar pasta tins of sardines and ice cream.
Greengrocer's:
apples pears bananas beans carrots and broccoli.
Baker's:
five bread rolls and two loaves of bread.
Hardware shop:
six short sturdy nails and a small hammer.

Comma commotion

There are too many commas in this cutting from a catalogue. Rewrite the descriptions, taking out 11 commas that should not be there.

These Cosifit ear muffs are warm, comfortable, and suitable for anyone from 6 to 60! The adjustable head strap means that however, big or small your head may be, Cosifit ear muffs, will always fit!

This latest addition to the Supertec, computer, game series is the most exciting, challenging and absorbing, yet! Can you help Hoghero in his desperate battle, for control of the universe? Help him stop nasty Miteymouse, from conquering the world!

Every trendy, teenager needs a Staralarm! When you go to bed, just set the alarm by choosing a time and a voice - the voice of your favourite, pop star. What better way to wake up than to the sound of Kool Malone, Freddy, and the Freezers, or Ritchy Roon?

Dot dot dot

You use three full stops in a row (...) to show that some words are missing, or that a sentence is unfinished:

I must not get these shoes...

Tinker, tailor, soldier... beggarman, thief.

You should not use three full stops after expressions such as *and so on* and *et cetera*. People sometimes do, but a single full stop here is correct.

Numbers

In maths, the full stop is used as the decimal point (as in *1.5* to mean *one and a half*). Always write the decimal point very clearly, as the difference between, for example, 1.5 and 15 is enormous.

In most written English, the comma is used to break up numbers that are over four figures long, for example, 10,000. You start from the right and put a comma in after each set of three numerals. This helps to make it easier to read long numbers. You do not normally do this in maths and science.

Comma tips

Page 38 explains how to use commas*. Sometimes, though, it is hard to decide where to put them. Here are two tips:

1 Make sure each complete sentence ends with a full stop, then try reading aloud, listening out for natural pauses. For each pause, think whether a comma is needed.
2 If you still do not know where to put the commas, perhaps your sentence is too complicated or too long, and needs rewriting.

Look at this example: *Mrs Fern, the head of my old school and the piano teacher who, years ago, gave my brother lessons, left to go to work in a circus.*

   In order to say that Mrs Fern, who is a former headmistress and piano teacher, went to work in a circus, you must rewrite the sentence. At present, because too many details are attached to the main information, the sentence could mean that Mrs Fern, the headmistress and the former piano teacher (three

different people) went to work in a circus. A comma before *and the teacher* will not help.
   Here is a possible rewrite: *Mrs Fern, who was the head of my old school and was also the piano teacher who, years ago, gave my brother lessons, left to go to work in a circus.*

To do the puzzles on these two pages, you may need to look back at pages 35 and 37.

Mix and match

Here are eight sentences, each cut in two. By looking at the capital letters, full stops and commas, see if you can match up the sixteen pieces to make the eight most suitable sentences.

but I still could not make up my mind.

, then grudgingly guided them down the dark alley.

After the detective's visit

I thought it over

In the late afternoon,

, which is in Canada.

and quickly decided on a course of action.

Andy and his parents have moved to Gap,

The woman looked down her nose at them,

He gave me some sound advice,

which is in France.

I decided to go to the police station.

, I no longer felt in the mood to work.

The man wrinkled up his nose in disdain

Jan and her family have moved to Arcola

but agreed to show them the documents.

*Commas are also used in letter writing (see page 56) and in direct speech, such as *I said, "Come back!"* (see page 52).

Stop gap

Copy out these sentences, using five full stops, eleven commas and a set of three dots (...) to complete them.

1 Live coverage of this fascinating sporting event will begin on Radio Livewire at 6

2 There were 18000 people at the concert so our chances of bumping into Gemma Jim and Sam were very slight

3 Disheartened the explorers began their return journey setting off

4 In early Roman times theatres were built of wood

5 At last wet gasping and exhausted they reached the bus shelter

6 The sun which we had not seen for two months blinded us

Printer problems

This printer prints three dots wherever a full stop or a comma is needed, as well as where three full stops are correct. Copy the text out, replacing the three dots with full stops and commas wherever you think would be best.

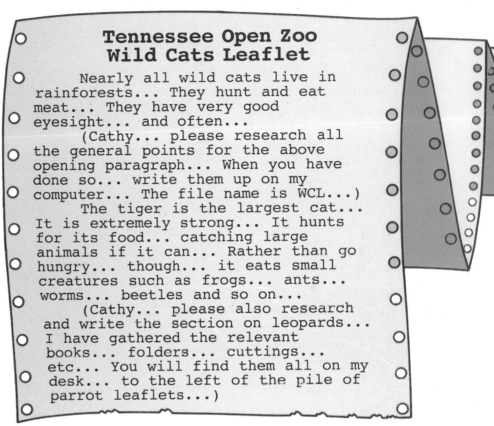

Tennessee Open Zoo Wild Cats Leaflet

Nearly all wild cats live in rainforests... They hunt and eat meat... They have very good eyesight... and often...

(Cathy... please research all the general points for the above opening paragraph... When you have done so... write them up on my computer... The file name is WCL...)

The tiger is the largest cat... It is extremely strong... It hunts for its food... catching large animals if it can... Rather than go hungry... though... it eats small creatures such as frogs... ants... worms... beetles and so on...

(Cathy... please also research and write the section on leopards... I have gathered the relevant books... folders... cuttings... etc... You will find them all on my desk... to the left of the pile of parrot leaflets...)

Hasty homework

This essay has full stops and capital letters, but no other punctuation. Copy it out, adding commas where needed (the photos may help you).

My summer holiday
For my summer holiday I went to Agadir a beach paradise in Morocco. I stayed in a luxury hotel with three enormous swimming pools a cinema two discos a jogging track and a computer games room.

The hotel is by a beautiful long white beach and the bedrooms which have balconies overlook the sea. My Mum and Dad had a hard time getting to sleep because of the waves crashing down below. My room which had no balcony and was just around the corner was quiet.

I did not like the pools as much as the sea although they did have lots of truly awesome water rapids waves and whirlpools. The two swimming pools which have lots of sun-loungers around them are always crowded. Because the third one has lanes in it for serious swimming it is usually empty. On the beach there were huge waves which I loved. One morning after a storm I saw some jellyfish on the beach.

The food was brilliant. The hotel has chefs from all over the world so we mostly ate Chinese food and Moroccan food which were our favourites.

Even though we only spent a day there our visit to Marrakesh was the highlight of the whole holiday. It is a really exciting town and the markets and tiny ancient streets are full of weird things like carpets olives and spices all piled up leather bags and sandals.

Because it was spring and the weather was not too hot I really enjoyed this holiday.

colon

Make sure you pack the following items: map, compass, torch, whistle and waterproof jacket.

semicolon

Rehearsing this piece of music is good fun; performing it in front of people is the problem.

The colon is two dots, one above the other. The semicolon is made of a dot over a comma. Both of them represent a pause in a sentence (a longer pause than shown by a comma and a shorter one than shown by a full stop). They are not followed by a capital letter.

The semicolon

This has two main uses:

1 It can separate two closely linked main clauses* of similar importance. It is used instead of a full stop or a word like *and* or *but*. For example: *He lifted the lid; the lost gems fell out.*

In this example, the semicolon gives a dramatic effect of short, linked pieces. Using a full stop instead, the effect would be jerky: *He lifted the lid. The lost gems fell out.* With *and*, it would be less dramatic: *He lifted the lid and the lost gems fell out.*

If using a semicolon seems tricky, just avoid it. A practical tip is to think of using one before words such as *besides*, *consequently*, *therefore*, *even so*, *still*, *otherwise* and *moreover* when these link two main clauses. For example: *Their train was late; even so, they got the connection.*

2 The semicolon is also used to break up the different items in a list.

Normally, you use commas for this (see page 38). But if the items in the list are long and complicated (which often means they need commas themselves), you use semicolons instead. For example: *To make this bag, you will need a large, sturdy needle for sewing tough fabrics; extremely thick thread made of nylon or some sort of synthetic material; coarse, rip-stop grey fabric with the logo printed on it; and finally, a white button of any sort**.*

The colon

The colon does two things:

1 It can introduce a list of items. For example: *To build a model train tunnel, you will need: a shoe box, sandpaper, paints and glue.* You can also write a list with no colon (...*you will need a shoe box, sandpaper...*). By drawing attention to the start of the list, the colon helps make the writing clear.

In two cases, the colon is essential:
a) when the list is laid out as a column.
You will need:
a shoe box
sandpaper
paints
glue.

b) when the list begins *You will need the following*: or *Here is a checklist of things you should do*: or expressions like this. In cases like these, you can tell that you need a colon before the start of the list itself because you cannot read on without a pause.

2 The colon can go between two main clauses to introduce an explanation or a summary of the first clause:
We soon solved the mystery of the missing sausages: the dog had helped himself. (explanation)
As she read the letter, she grinned and hugged everyone: she was over the moon with joy. (summary)

*This is the part of a sentence that contains a subject and a verb, and which makes sense on its own.
**Here a semicolon is used before *and finally*, but a comma would be possible instead.

Fishy prizes

Here are the three winning entries in a cookery competition. To make the recipes clear, where in each one should you add two colons, a comma and a semicolon?

First Prize

Quiche Marine – For the pastry, you will need flour, butter or margarine, one egg.

For the filling, have ready the following fresh prawns, shelled; crab meat either fresh or from a tin cream, eggs and seasoning.

Make the pastry in the usual way, roll it out and line a flan dish with it. Mix the ingredients for the filling, pour them onto the pastry and bake for 25 minutes.

Second Prize

Perfect Fish Pie – To make the potato layer, mix together some mashed potatoes, milk and eggs.

For the fish layer, get the following mixture ready: chopped fresh plaice, sole and salmon in equal quantities. Mix these together, adding a dash of salt and a squeeze of lemon juice.

The ingredients for the cheese sauce are equal amounts of milk, cream and yogurt; a tablespoon of flour; finely grated cheddar cheese; two beaten egg yolks. Stir these together in a pan, heating gently until thick. Don't include the cheese this must go in after the sauce has thickened and is off the heat.

To assemble the pie do the following: put half the potato in the bottom of an ovenproof dish; place the fish mixture on top, making sure it is well spread over all the potato; cover with the remaining potato finally, pour the cheese sauce over the top and bake for 30 minutes. Serve with a green salad.

Young Chef of the Month

A prize for entries from cooks aged 11 or under.

Green Fishcakes with Pink Sauce – For the fishcakes, mash together these ingredients poached cod, boiled potatoes and two raw eggs. Add a mixture of finely chopped fresh herbs. Include parsley and chives, and one of the following dill, fennel, sorrel. Also add a knob of butter. Shape this mixture into fishcakes and fry gently in a little butter and corn oil.

For the sauce mince some peeled shrimps and mix with lots of sour cream.

When the fishcakes are ready, heat the sauce and pour it into the plates. Place the fishcakes on top of the sauce. As a main course, serve with boiled new potatoes and broccoli as a starter, serve with crusty bread.

Getting it right

Copy out these ads, adding either a colon or a semicolon to each.

Washomatic for sale. This machine is a genuine bargain: it is only 12 years old; there is not a single visible patch of rust on it last but not least, it does not leak. Phone Johnny on 324 5543.

Attention, old pen collectors! Green Silhouette pen for sale, 1952 model. Features included original case, gold nib, embossed logo. Phone Pipa Pentop, 324 5682.

For sale or hire garage in Bach Alley. Contact Mrs Lucas, 3 Bach Square.

WANTED YOUNG PERSON TO DELIVER NEWSPAPERS IN COMBE PARK AREA. MUST HAVE OWN BIKE. APPLY TO NAT'S NEWS.

Gardener sought. The following qualifications are required familiarity with Supermow, sound knowledge of organic vegetable growing and garden pest control. Phone 324 3344.

Hair excesses

Copy out these pieces of writing, taking out the surplus punctuation. Each one has an unnecessary colon or semicolon.

Come to us: for a wide range of hair care: perms, hair straightening, colour change, highlights, beading, hair extensions.

Our perms are perfect in every way: gentle, lasting; and adapted to suit your face shape.

Choose between three wonderful shampoos: frosted yogurt and banana for dry hair; lemon and lime cocktail for greasy hair; finally, for problem hair, mango and chilli revitalizing magic; or Brazil nut balsam.

Always follow up a shampoo with a good conditioner: this guarantees good hair condition. Amongst our dozens of choices, we recommend either: deep action strawberry, marigold petal extract or luxury oatmilk.

Treat yourself to: a head massage, the ideal treatment for tired heads. You get a 15 minute massage given by an expert; generous amounts of the best massage oils; a shampoo and blow dry.

We give you the hair shape you want. Once you have it, you will want to keep it; to help you, we stock 30 varieties of hair spray. Also in stock: hundreds of lacquers, hair gels; and waxes.

43

The question mark is a sign that goes on the end of a sentence which asks a question. It shows where, in speech, you would raise your voice a little, then pause as for a full stop.

Can you hear me?

question mark

Direct questions

The kind of question which ends with a question mark is called a direct question. It is a question to which an answer is expected. This is how typical direct questions look:

| They begin with a capital letter. |

Are you tired?*

| first word is a verb or a question word (see right) | | subject comes after the verb |

Why are you tired?

| They end with a question mark. |

Longer questions may begin with extra words, but the order (verb/subject or question word/verb/subject) is the same. For example: *So then, why are you tired?*

Direct questions can be very short and have no verb or subject. For example: *Why?*

As the question mark is used instead of a full stop, you put a capital letter after it: *Why are you tired? It is only ten o'clock.*

Indirect questions

An indirect question is a type of sentence which looks a little like a direct question but is a normal sentence. It ends with a full stop, not a question mark. Here is an example: *She is asking if you can hear.*

It is a sentence which tells you about a question that was asked. You can think of it as a reported question.

To spot an indirect question, look for expressions like *ask* or *wonder* used with *if, whether* or a question word (see above right). Notice too that the word order is subject/verb (*you can*), not the other way around (*can you*) as for a direct question.

Question words

Here are the most commonly used question words:

Whose? Whom? Where? Why? What? Who? When? Which? How?

Some of these words are not used only in questions. They can double up as other kinds of words. For example: *When I was on the ferry, I felt ill.*

Question tags

Question tags are short and are tagged onto the end of a statement, after a comma: *You play the violin, don't you?* These question tags belong to spoken English, so avoid them in formal writing such as essays. However, if you write one, remember that it turns the sentence into a question, so put a question mark on the end.

——Ask a straight question——

How many of the following are direct questions that need a question mark, and how many are indirect ones that don't?

1 **I asked her if she could bring him to my party**
2 **Can you bring your brother to my party**
3 **Does anyone know where I put my watch**
4 **Is there a sweet shop around here**
5 **Did you ask if there is a sweet shop around here**
6 **When do you think you will be able to help out on the school magazine**
7 **Will you be able to help out on the school magazine**
8 **Who do you feel we could invite along**

44

*In very informal, spoken English, questions are sometimes made without moving the verb: *You're tired?* If you write down a question like this, for example in a note, put a question mark on the end.

Awkward questions

Each of the ten questions on this police report have been printed in jumbled order. Can you work out what the questions might be? (They are all direct questions.)

1. live you here Do?

2. night were eleven Where at o'clock last you?

3. with who TV are of friends were What watching the the you names four ?

4. unusual Did your you friends or of anything hear one?

5. you friend a Jack have Do called?

6. night here Was last he?

7. heard around you who the Gang, gang the Have a of of hang Burly thugs neighbourhood?

8. their them you to leader or Jack ever about Hasn't boasted mentioned being?

9. heard unusual if asked when Why lie I you you you had anything did?

10. so it Was Jack you he parents' night who could gave your garage key to hide there the last?

Searching questions

Help Jan enter a songwriting competition. Copy the lyrics she has written, adding full stops or question marks to the ends of the seven lines that need them.

One day, you'll leave, won't you
When I asked you last summer,
You said you'd be true,
But now, I just wonder

Why is it always me
That gets left behind
In this state, I can't see
How life can ever be kind

Friends are no better
Why are they never around
When I need a shoulder
Oh, when will I stop feeling so blue

Questionnaire mix-up

Sam has written a list of questions which form a character questionnaire. They run on, one after the other, but have got mixed up with other, incorrectly punctuated pieces. Can you pick the right line, from each batch of three, to follow from the previous one?

1. a) How old are

2. a) the boys in the team. How would you describe
   b) you? How would you describe
   c) your two sisters, would you describe

3. a) yourself? Are you
   b) yourself and your sister. Are you
   c) your best friend. Is she

4. a) generous or selfish. I wonder whether you feel
   b) mean and difficult, We wonder if you like
   c) lively or quiet? We wonder if you like

5. a) jeans or skirts best. Are
   b) red or pink nail polish best? Are
   c) country and western music? Are

6. a) your eyes blue
   b) you short or tall.
   c) your eyes dark or light.

7. a) green or hazel? Can you
   b) , green or hazel? Can you
   c) green or hazel. Can you

8. a) tell me how how often you play tennis. Do you like
   b) ride a bike. Do you enjoy
   c) swim, play tennis and ride a bike? You enjoy

9. a) playing the piano, don't you? Do you prefer
   b) playing the piano, don't you... Do you prefer
   c) playing the piano? Do you prefer

10. a) sports to quiet things like reading.
    b) playing computer games or watching TV?
    c) playing computer, games or watching TV?

45

I'm scared!

exclamation mark

The exclamation mark is a vertical line over a dot. It can go on the end of a sentence instead of a full stop. An exclamation mark shows that the sentence expresses a strong feeling such as anger, delight, surprise or fear.

When do you use one?

Exclamation marks are optional. You can always end the type of sentence described above with a full stop.

There is no rule about this. The best advice is to use few exclamation marks. If you use too many, they have less effect. Use one on the end of short expressions (such as *Ouch!*), and where you want to draw attention to the strength of feeling.

Look at this example: *What a storm! It was unbelievable! The thunder and lightning were continuous, the sky was black and the rain came down in torrents! Within seconds, we were soaked! I have never been so scared!*

With fewer exclamation marks, the effect is stronger: *What a storm! It was unbelievable. The thunder and lightning were continuous, the sky was black and the rain came down in torrents. Within seconds, we were soaked. I have never been so scared.*

Where you place exclamation marks changes the meaning slightly by drawing attention to the sentences that have them. In this piece of writing, you could underline the scary effect of the storm by putting one on the end: *I have never been so scared!*

Short expressions

A tip for dealing with more than one expression of surprise, anger and so on is to use a mixture of commas and exclamation marks. For example, you should avoid writing *Wow! How brilliant!* Instead, write *Wow, how brilliant!*

It can also go on the end of an order or a short expression to show that they are said loudly or with lots of feeling:

Ouch!

What a stupid thing to do!

Call the police!

Remember, as the exclamation mark is used instead of a full stop, it is followed by a capital letter.

One only

Where you want an exclamation mark, one is always enough. You may see two or three used, but you should only use one.

——— **Overkill** ———

Copy this newspaper article, cutting eight exclamation points and replacing two of these with commas. (Adjust capital letters as necessary.)

What a calamity!!! Dire is to lose its railway station toilet unless urgent action is taken. This, at least, is what the Association of Dire Residents (ADR) fear, following their meeting with the Station's Passenger Liaison Committee (SPLC) yesterday.

According to the ADR spokesperson, Gail Bigwail, the Committee is intent on cutting costs. Losing the toilet will save exactly the amount they are looking for.

What an unnecessary, backwards step!! The shortest journey from Dire is 23 minutes, and with no toilet at Dire Central, passengers would just have to keep their legs crossed!!!

We agree with Ivor Right, also of the ADR, who points out that, with a little thought and care, small savings could be made here and there, thus allowing the toilet to be kept open. How true, Mr. Right, and how eagerly we will publicize your views! The ADR are planning a Day of Action in the near future. So cheer up, Citizens of Dire! Buy the Dire Echo every day! And we will keep you informed!!

Surprise, surprise

Dawn has come top in her class this year. Her little brother took all the messages she received and scratched out some of the punctuation. Each message should have an extra exclamation mark, comma and full stop. Copy the four messages, adding the right punctuation in each of the scratched spaces.

Foxes' Dale
Boarding School for Boys

Wow, you HAVE got a brain after all ⚡
I suppose I'm impressed ⚡ though it's pretty horrid having to admit it ⚡
See you on Saturday, Einstein.
Charlie

Great stuff, Miss Brainypants ⚡ After Lady Banstead's stunning announcement ⚡ I can only beg to remain your proud best friend ⚡
See you at volleyball, clever socks!
Di

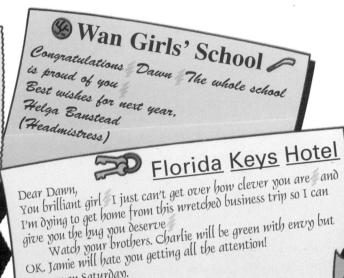

Wan Girls' School

Congratulations ⚡ Dawn ⚡ The whole school is proud of you ⚡
Best wishes for next year,
Helga Banstead
(Headmistress)

Florida Keys Hotel

Dear Dawn,
You brilliant girl ⚡ I just can't get over how clever you are ⚡ and I'm dying to get home from this wretched business trip so I can give you the hug you deserve ⚡
Watch your brothers. Charlie will be green with envy but OK. Jamie will hate you getting all the attention!
See you on Saturday.
Lots of love,
Mum

Fruit machine roundup

This puzzle gives you a chance to test yourself on all the punctuation explained so far in this book (from page 35 to here).

Someone has played on the fruit machine and jumbled the last two parts of each sentence. Copy the first pieces, then work out which centre pieces and which end pieces match up with them. (Look closely at the punctuation.)

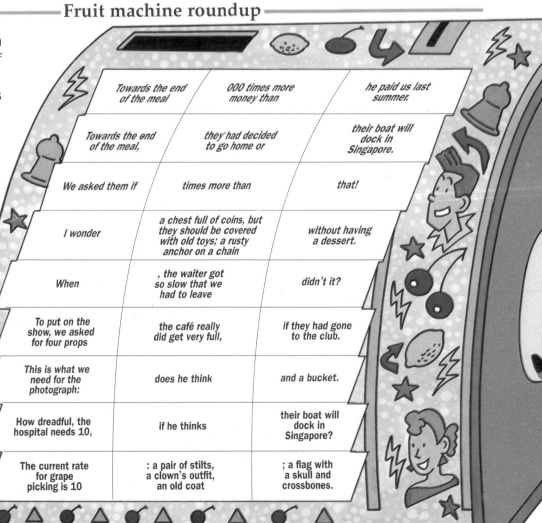

Towards the end of the meal	000 times more money than	he paid us last summer.
Towards the end of the meal,	they had decided to go home or	their boat will dock in Singapore.
We asked them if	times more than	that!
I wonder	a chest full of coins, but they should be covered with old toys; a rusty anchor on a chain	without having a dessert.
When	, the waiter got so slow that we had to leave	didn't it?
To put on the show, we asked for four props	the café really did get very full,	if they had gone to the club.
This is what we need for the photograph:	does he think	and a bucket.
How dreadful, the hospital needs 10,	if he thinks	their boat will dock in Singapore?
The current rate for grape picking is 10	: a pair of stilts, a clown's outfit, an old coat	; a flag with a skull and crossbones.

The apostrophe looks like a comma, but it goes higher on the line. The top of it lines up with the tops of letters like *l* and *k*.

apostrophe

Annie's cat is at the door.

Two uses

The apostrophe is used in two ways:
1 It can show that some letters are missing (as in *The cat's at the door*, where *cat's* stands for *cat is*). This is explained on page 50.
2 It can also show possession (who something belongs to), as in the example, *Annie's cat*.

's for possession

To show who something belongs to, you normally add *'s* to the owner's name. Here are some examples of this possessive *'s*:

Fred's shirt (the shirt that belongs to Fred, or the shirt of Fred)

the teacher's car (the car that belongs to the teacher, or the car of the teacher)

King Midas's gold (the gold belonging to King Midas, or the gold of King Midas)

the actress's wig (the wig belonging to the actress, or the wig of the actress)

This *'s* is correct for all nouns (naming words) when they are singular. Singular means there is only one, as opposed to plural (more than one). For example, *car* is singular (only one), and *cars* is plural (more than one). Look at the examples above and notice that even singular nouns which end in *s* add *'s*.

Plural nouns

Most nouns have an extra *s* on the end when they are plural (more than one). For example: *parents*. To show possession for these, you add only an apostrophe*. Here are some examples:
my parents' car (the car that belongs to my parents)
the Smiths' car (the car that belongs to the Smiths)

Unusual plurals

A few nouns do not have an extra *s* or *es* when they are plural, but change in another way. For example: *child, children*. To show possession for these, add *'s*. For example: *the children's room*.

Spotting possessives

To tell if a noun with an *s* needs an apostrophe, try using *of*. For example, for *Annie's cat*, you can say the *cat of Annie*. This means it is possessive and needs *'s*.

——————— **Filling the gap** ———————

For these sentences, which word shown in blue fits the gap?

1 His ... house is in Armadillo.
parents'/parents
2 Their ... bedrooms are all in the attic.
children's/childrens'
3 We ended up in the ... worst restaurant.
towns/town's/towns'
4 My ... colours are scarlet, blue and yellow.
teams/teams'/team's
5 My favourite ... annual tour starts next week.
bands/band's/bands'
6 Mrs ... next-door neighbour is a retired filmstar.
Jones/Jones's
7 Of this ... two radios, only one is working.
ship's/ships'/ships's
8 The conductor would not let us onto the ... top deck.
buses'/bus's
9 By the end of the match, the 13 ... energy had completely run out.
player's/players'/players
10 The ... garage had been emptied overnight.
Brown's/Browns'

*For nouns which end in *ch*, *sh*, *s*, *x* or *z*, and a few which end in *o*, add *es*. For some of those ending in *y*, the *y* changes to *i* and you add *es*. For example: *bush, bushes; baby, babies*.

Get the facts right

Look at the words and pictures below. For the first set, the correct phrase is *the cats' basket*. Add apostrophes to make the remaining eleven phrases. Make sure that the nouns in your phrases change to plural where necessary to match the pictures.

1 cat   basket

2 woman   umbrella

3 hamster   carrot

4 cook   spoon

5 policeman motorbike

6 girl   sandwich

7 friend   surfboard

8 mouse   hole

9 butcher   knife

10 dog   bone

11 thief   bag

12 boy   CD player

Photo album

Of the two sentences given for each photo, only one matches the picture. Can you work out which?

A1 My cousins' hair is jet black.
A2 My cousin's hair is jet black.

B1 The girl's room is blue.
B2 The girls' room is blue.

C1 My uncles' vans are purple.
C2 My uncle's vans are purple.

D1 All the baby's clothes are stripy.
D2 All the babies' clothes are stripy.

E1 My aunt's eyes are green.
E2 My aunts' eyes are green.

F1 Their dogs' bowls are yellow.
F2 Their dog's bowls are yellow.

49

When you write the words that someone said, you use quotation marks to show where their words begin and end*. The opening marks look like two upside-down apostrophes. The closing ones look like two apostrophes. Quotation marks are also quite often called speech marks, inverted commas or quotes.

John said, "They've quotation found the way out." marks

All about direct speech

Direct speech is when you write spoken words in quotation marks. The words go inside the quotation marks with their punctuation, though you sometimes have to adjust the punctuation a little.

The verb that introduces the spoken words (*say, ask, whisper* and so on) can go first, last, or in the middle. Here you can see how the punctuation should be in each case:

1 If the verb is first:

> two capital letters: one at the start of the sentence, and one where the spoken words start

He said, "They've found the way out."

> comma* at the end of the introduction, before "

> full stop before "

2 If the verb is last:

> one capital letter only

"They've found the way out," he said.

> comma after the spoken words, before " (replacing the full stop that the spoken words ended with)

3 If the verb is in the middle:

> comma within the quotation marks

"From what I can see," he said, peering into the binoculars, "they've found the way out."

> comma before "

> one full stop at the end, before "

Think of the words in quotation marks and the words that introduce them as a sentence. Whichever of the three patterns you follow, the sentence starts with a capital letter and ends with a full stop (or *?* or *!*). If the closing quotation marks are on the end (as in 1 and 3), the full stop (or *?* or *!*) is within them.

Ending with ? and !

If the spoken words end with a question mark or exclamation mark, this is what you do:
He asked, "Have you found the way out?"
He said, "They've found the way out!"

> ? or ! before " (no need for a full stop)

"Have you found the way out?" he asked.
"They've found the way out!" he said.

> no capital letter after ? or ! (notice that this breaks the usual rule about having a capital letter after ! and ?)

Dialogue

When you write a dialogue (two or more people's spoken words), you can start a new paragraph (see page 60) each time you switch to a new speaker. This helps to make clear who is speaking:

"Who did you say?" she asked.
"I said Fred, but I meant Ted!" he answered, laughing.

Indirect speech

There is another way of writing people's words, called indirect, or reported, speech. This is when you report the words that someone said, rather than giving their exact spoken words. For example: *John said that they had found the way out.* In indirect speech, you never use quotation marks.

*A colon is sometimes used here instead of the comma: *He said: "They've found the way out."*

What was that?

Write what these six people are saying, using direct speech. For each one, start with *he* or *she said* (or *he* or *she asked*, in the case of questions). Then do the same again, but put *he/she said* or *he/she asked* at the end. Try to get all the punctuation right.

Right, put your pens down now, please!

Carol's taken my pen.

Jamie was copying Tracy's answers.

I can't believe how hard that was!

Did you hear about Ros and Kate?

I've left my lunch box at home!

Adventure diary

In total, there are 12 sets of quotation marks missing from these diary entries. Read them through, then copy out all the sections that need quotation marks, adding these in (and adjusting the punctuation to go with them).

Great Rocks Holiday Centre

Day 1

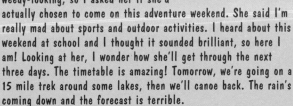

Now I'm here, I'm sure I shall be all right. Everyone's really friendly and no one looks the real outdoors type. I'm sharing a room with a girl called Claire.

We chatted a bit before this evening's meal. She is thin, pale and weedy-looking, so I asked her if she'd actually chosen to come on this adventure weekend. She said I'm really mad about sports and outdoor activities. I heard about this weekend at school and I thought it sounded brilliant, so here I am! Looking at her, I wonder how she'll get through the next three days. The timetable is amazing! Tomorrow, we're going on a 15 mile trek around some lakes, then we'll canoe back. The rain's coming down and the forecast is terrible.

Day 2

The day was so full, Claire and I still didn't get a chance to chat much. When we were setting off this morning, Alice, our instructor, asked her why is your backpack twice the size of everyone else's? My strange room-mate answered because I want to get really fit! Alice said leave a few things behind. Claire just shook her head and laughed.

I'm too tired to stay up writing about it all. Tomorrow we're going to do some climbing and abseiling. Aaagh!

Day 3

Well, the weekend is nearly over. Tonight, we're going to have a barbecue by the lake. Today was awesome. The abseiling was just as scary as I'd thought, and when it was all over, Alice told me you'll have to come back with Claire in the summer. You make a great team! When I asked her why, she said you're over-cautious but Claire encourages you. Claire's reckless but you keep her in check.

At the barbecue, I got a chance to talk to Claire a bit more. She's amazing. I love doing all this she told me while we were stuffing our faces because I broke an arm and a leg in a skiing accident last winter and I got so fed up having to stay indoors all the time.

Home again

How was your weekend? everyone keeps asking me. I just say I was best at everything. You know me! What I don't tell them about is the nightmares I keep having.

A few hours after I'd got home, Claire phoned to ask if I want to go back to Great Rocks with her in August. Well I answered I'll think about it and phone you back soon. Whoops, I don't have her phone number!

53

I stepped across the fast-running stream (as the picture shows).

brackets   hyphen

There is no room left — I said: no room!

dash

Brackets

Brackets are pairs of curved lines which you use around words in order to separate them from the rest of a sentence.
For example:
My ant project is finished, but Jan's Dad (an insect specialist, as I found out) said he would look at it before I hand it in.

Usually, the words in brackets give extra detail or an explanation.

With brackets, the punctuation depends on whether you choose to write the words in brackets as part of a sentence or as a separate sentence.

If they are part of a sentence, any punctuation that belongs to the sentence goes outside the brackets. For example:
Entries must reach us by 22 May (any received later will not be valid).

If they form a separate sentence, the punctuation goes inside the brackets:
Entries must reach us by 22 May. (Entries received later will not be valid.)

Dashes

A dash is a short horizontal line used on its own or as part of a pair**. It is best avoided, especially in formal writing.

Dashes have about the same use as brackets. In informal writing or in direct speech, you can use them instead of brackets. Use two dashes if the extra words are in the middle of the sentence, as in *They want to visit Paris — I can see why — on their way to Geneva*. Use one dash if the extra words are at the end: *They want to visit Paris — I can understand why.*

Hyphens

A hyphen is like a dash, but shorter. Its main use is to join two or more words to show they should be read as one word with its own meaning. For example: *on-the-spot fines, short-term deal.*

Words like this, made from two or more words, are called compound words. Some gradually become accepted as new words that you write without a hyphen, For example: *offside, seaweed, flashback.*

There are no firm rules to tell you when to join words up or when to link them with hyphens. You will often have to check compound words in a dictionary.

Hyphen guidelines

1   Use hyphens if the meaning is unclear or wrong without them:
A   *two-month-old kittens*
B   *two month-old kittens*

2   Use hyphens to join words that must be read as one and that are before a noun they describe: *a long-overdue award.*
3   Use a hyphen to join a verb ending in *ing* or *ed* with another word that changes its meaning. For example: *well-tuned, mind-boggling*. (The exception is if the other word ends in *ly*, when no hyphen is needed: *nicely worded.*)
4   Use a hyphen to join words with the same last and first letters: *grass-seed.*

In American English, more compound words are written as one word than in British English. For example: *night-time* (UK) but *nighttime* (US).

Other uses

The hyphen is used to mean *to* in expressions like *1964-1982.*

Hyphens also go on the end of a line to break up a long word for which there is not enough room. Avoid this in your writing if you can. If you do it, break the word in a place which will not make reading difficult.

It is a pa-ragraph.   It is a para-graph.

*You can often use commas instead of brackets. Use brackets when they make the writing much clearer, as in this example.
**Never use other punctuation next to a dash.

Pirates aboard game

The story below has 19 numbered gaps. Use the board on the right to complete it. For each gap, look at the strip with the matching number and select the correct piece to fill the gap. (You will probably have to look some words up in a dictionary.)

Pirate MacClaw crept up the 1 to the galleon's deck. 2 Tom Puffin, who had rowed old MacClaw across from the 3 pirate ship 4 sick with fear all the way), shivered in the boat beneath.

5 MacClaw (who had celebrated his 6 the previous night) ran across the deserted deck towards the captain's quarters. He did not blink an 7 as he caught sight of the huge cages in which the galleon's captain was reputed to keep 8 and a 9 tiger. He had other things on his mind.

Soon he was creeping into Captain Cachou's cabin 10 was fast asleep on a 11 stool opposite the door. Unfortunately, MacClaw's parrot (who had been 12 on the old pirate's left shoulder ever since he had clambered on board the galleon) suddenly screeched, "Pirate MacClaw here!" This 13 went unheard, though, for the captain was in his 14 and his head was 15.

In the 16, the pirate had the 17 leather folder firmly in his large hands and was running back down towards Tom. The boy quietly sighed with relief (and wondered how he would ever have his 18 Mission accomplished, Tom rowed them into the peaceful, safe darkness, in which the blurred outlines of the 19 soon appeared.

MacCLAW'S MISSION

1	loosely tied rope ladder	loosely-tied rope-ladder	loosely tied ropeladder
2	Mean while	Mean-while	Meanwhile,
3	nowinvisible	now invisible	now-invisible
4	(and who had felt	and who had felt	and (who had felt
5	Quietfooted	Quiet-footed	Quiet footed
6	seventieth birthday	seventieth birth day	seventieth birth-day
7	eye lid	eye-lid	eyelid
8	blood-hounds	bloodhounds	blood hounds
9	maneating	man eating	man-eating
10	— the guard	(the guard	— the guard —
11	three legged	threelegged	three-legged
12	solidly-perched	solidly perched	solidlyperched
13	ill timed squawk	illtimed squawk	ill-timed squawk
14	bathtub	bath-tub	bath tub
15	under water	under-water	underwater
16	twinkling of an eye	twinkling-of-an-eye	twinkling of an eye —
17	longdesired	long-desired	long desired
18	grand-pa's courage).	grandpa's courage.)	grandpa's courage).
19	pirate ship	pirate-ship	pirateship

Face painting

Where should you add one pair of brackets in each of these seven instructions?

1. You will need face paints, two or three brushes and at least one sponge see Getting started on p.1.

2. Use water-based paints they cost more but give better results.

3. Sponge a yellow base onto the face brownish yellow if possible.

4. Sponge a white muzzle and chin lions have a white beard.

5. Paint a black nose joined to a black upper lip; also paint black lines around the eyes. See the illustration.

6. Paint bottom lip red and add black whiskers dots and lines as shown.

7. Brush hair up and back into a mane and sponge white streaks onto it. These will easily wash out.

If the layout of your writing (the way it is placed on the page) is cramped, it is hard to read. Here are some guidelines to help you present it neatly. You can also find out how to lay out letters.

Margins

Margins are the spaces which you leave on the left and right with no writing in them.

The left-hand margin should be straight (you can draw a line in with a ruler), and it is often a little wider than the right-hand margin. You can make the right-hand margin straight too, although you may end up with awkward gaps between the words.

Each new paragraph starts at the same distance from the left-hand margin.

Someone had to go down. The divers all looked terrified. Titch volunteered.

She lowered herself into the sea and let go of the ladder. She soon located the wreck, a gloomy shape beneath her. She found the right porthole. It was shut tight.

She tugged on the frame. All of a sudden, it was pushed from inside. An unknown diver's face appeared.

Paragraphs

A paragraph is a short section of writing within a longer piece. Each new paragraph starts a little way from the left margin (called indenting).

There are no rules to say where you should start a new paragraph. Usually, you do so when you move to a new subject or a new aspect of the same subject.

Formal letters

There are two styles to choose from.

Style 1: indented paragraphs

Address of person you are writing to

your address

Fun Products,
4 Creek Road,
London, SE8 3PH
10 July 1997

Mr Jensen,
The Magic Shop,
36 Park Avenue,
Barmouth,
Gwynedd, GW7 2PL

date

comma (*Dear Sir* or *Dear Madam* if you don't know the name)*

Dear Mr Jensen,
On 6 June, I sent you a sample of our latest false moustache.
Please either let me know your response or return the sample to me.
Yours sincerely,
Katie Katz
Katie Katz

Sign, and type or write your name clearly.

Style 2: everything lined up on the left, except your address**

Fun Products,
4 Creek Road,
London, SE8 3PH
10 July 1997

Mr Jensen,
The Magic Shop,
36 Park Avenue,
Barmouth,
Gwynedd, GW7 2PL

Dear Mr Jensen,
On 6 June, I sent you a sample of our latest false moustache.

Please either let me know your response or return the sample to me.
Yours sincerely,
Katie Katz
Katie Katz

Leave a little space between paragraphs.

Informal letters

For letters to friends or family, you can follow either style. You leave out the person's address, though, and you could also leave out your own. End with something like *With love from*, *See you soon* or *With best wishes*:

*7 Mermaid Lane,
Rye,
East Sussex,
Tuesday 12 August*

*Dear Ben,
The week in Dorset was brilliant. Many thanks once again for organizing it.
Did you find Lucy's lead? I'm sure I left it in your car. Please bring it down on Sunday.
Love to you all,
Ray*

Envelopes

There are two possible styles for the address on an envelope:

Mr Jensen,
The Magic Shop,
36 Park Avenue,
Barmouth,
Gwynedd, GW7 2PL.

Mr Jensen,
The Magic Shop,
36 Park Avenue,
Barmouth,
Gwynedd, GW7 2PL.

Addresses

On the letters and envelopes shown here, all the addresses have commas. This punctuation can be left out, even in formal letters.

*If you don't know whether you are writing to a man or woman, put *Dear Sir/Madam*. In this case, end with *Yours faithfully*.
**Notice that this breaks the usual rule about starting new paragraphs away from the left margin.

Letter box

Lay out these two letters properly. Do letter 1 following style 1 and letter 2 following style 2 (see opposite page).

Letter 1

Date: 7 May 1997
From: you (at your own address)
To: the manager of an ice-rink. You know the manager is a man, but you don't know his name.
The ice-rink's address: Ice World, Coldharbour Street, London N4 1RT.
What your letter says (write it in a single paragraph): I came skating yesterday and I left my shoes in the changing room. Please keep them for me if you find them. I will pick them up next week.

Letter 2

Date: 6 May 1997
From: you (at your own address)
To: Mrs Graham, the manageress of a supermarket.
The supermarket's address: Cheapstore, 106 Kiln Road, Birmingham BH7 6AJ.
What your letter says (break this into two paragraphs): Last week, I bought a jar of instant coffee from Cheapstore which I had to return. The coffee had a thick layer of green mould on the top. Please could you contact me about this matter as soon as possible? You said that I would hear from you within 48 hours, but I still have not.

Tiebreaker

To win trips to a city of their choice, the entrants in this competition had to give their reasons for wanting to go there. Here are the three winning entries. Can you split each one into three paragraphs?

Tiebreaker Competition

The city I most want to visit is Cairo. This is because the Sphinx and the Pyramids are just on the outskirts, and I would like to see them. I did a project on ancient Egypt and I built a model of the Sphinx. My model is small and new. I would like to stand in front of the real Sphinx, which is huge and ancient. Another reason for going to Cairo is to see the Nile. This is the longest river in the world, and if I visited Cairo, I could walk across it, using a bridge of course!

My best friend has moved to London, and my biggest hobby is history. Because of this, I want to visit London. My friend lives near the British Museum. He says it is full of exciting things to see, and wants to show me some seventh century Anglo-Saxon treasure there. I only know London from books. I would especially love to visit the Tower and the Houses of Parliament.

I am fascinated by buildings and one day I want to become an architect. I live on a cattle ranch in Oregon and I have never seen any tall buildings. The city I most want to visit is New York. Here I would see some of the oldest and most famous skyscrapers in the world. I could also see the wonderful skyline that they make. I have been saving my pocket money to go to New York for three years, but I still have not got enough. I hope I win this competition, because then I can go right away and I can buy a camera with the money I have saved.

57

Page 39 continued

Comma commotion

These Cosifit ear muffs are warm, **comfortable and** suitable for anyone from 6 to 60! The adjustable head strap means that **however big** or small your head may be, Cosifit ear **muffs will** always fit!

This latest addition to the **Supertec computer game** series is the most exciting, challenging and **absorbing yet!** Can you help Hoghero in his desperate **battle for** control of the universe? Help him stop **Miteymouse from** conquering the world!

Every **trendy teenager** needs a Staralarm! When you go to bed, just set the alarm by choosing a time and a voice - the voice of your **favourite pop** star. What better way to wake up than to the sound of Kool Malone, **Freddy** and the Freezers or Ritchy Roon?

Pages 40-41

Mix and match

Andy and his parents have moved to Gap,/ which is in France.

Jan and her family have moved to Arcola/, which is in Canada.

I thought it over/ and quickly decided on a course of action.

He gave me some sound advice,/ but I still could not make up my mind.

In the late afternoon,/ I decided to go to the police station.

After the detective's visit/, I no longer felt in the mood to work.

The man wrinkled up his nose in disdain/, then grudgingly guided them down the dark alley.

The woman looked down her nose at them,/ but agreed to show them the documents.

Stop gap

1 Live coverage of this fascinating sporting event will begin on Radio Livewire **at 6**.
2 There were **18,000** people at the **concert**, so our chances of bumping into **Gemma**, Jim and Sam were very **slight**.
3 **Disheartened**, the explorers began their return **journey**, setting **off...**
4 In early Roman **times**, theatres were built of **wood**.
5 At **last, wet**, gasping and **exhausted**, they reached the bus **shelter**.
6 The **sun**, which we had not seen for two **months**, blinded **us**.

Printer problems

Nearly all wild cats live in **rainforests**. They hunt and eat **meat**. They have very good **eyesight**, and often...

(**Cathy,** please research all the general points for the above opening **paragraph**. When you have done **so, write** them up on my **computer**. The file name is **WCL**.)

The tiger is the largest **cat**. It is extremely **strong**. It hunts for its **food**, catching large animals if it **can**. Rather than go **hungry, though,** it eats small creatures such as **frogs, ants, worms,** beetles and so on.

(**Cathy,** please also research and write the section on **leopards**. I have gathered the relevant **books, folders, cuttings,** etc. You will find them all on my **desk**, to the left of the pile of parrot **leaflets**.)

Hasty homework

For my summer **holiday**, I went to **Agadir**, a beach paradise in Morocco. I stayed in a luxury hotel with three enormous swimming **pools**, a **cinema**, two **discos**, a jogging track and a computer games room.

The hotel is by a **beautiful, long**, white beach (OR beautiful long white beach) and the bedrooms which have balconies overlook the sea. My Mum and Dad had a hard time getting to sleep because of the waves crashing down below. My **room**, which had no balcony and was just around the **corner**, was quiet.

I did not like the pools as much as the **sea**, although they did have lots of truly awesome water **rapids**, waves and whirlpools. The two swimming pools which have lots of sun-loungers around them are always crowded. Because the third one has lanes in it for serious **swimming**, it is usually empty. On the **beach**, there were huge waves, which I loved. One morning after a **storm**, I saw some jellyfish on the beach.

The food was brilliant. The hotel has chefs from all over the **world**, so we mostly ate Chinese food and Moroccan **food**, which were our favourites.

Even though we only spent a day **there**, our visit to Marrakesh was the highlight of the whole holiday. It is a really exciting **town**, and the markets and tiny ancient streets (OR **tiny**, ancient streets) are full of weird things like **carpets**, olives and spices all piled **up**, leather bags and sandals.

Because it was spring and the weather was not too **hot**, I really enjoyed this holiday.

Page 43

Fishy prizes

For the pastry, you will **need:** flour, butter [...]
For the filling, have ready the **following:** fresh prawns, shelled; crab **meat,** either fresh or from a **tin;** cream, eggs and seasoning. [...]

[...] The ingredients for the cheese sauce **are:** equal amounts of milk, cream and yogurt; a tablespoon of flour; finely grated cheddar cheese; two beaten egg yolks. Stir these [...] Don't include the **cheese:** this must go in after the sauce has thickened and is off the heat. To assemble the **pie,** do the following: put half the potato in the bottom of an ovenproof dish; place the fish mixture on top, making sure it is well spread over all the potato; cover with the remaining **potato;** finally, pour the cheese sauce [...]
For the fishcakes, mash together these **ingredients:** poached cod, boiled potatoes and two raw eggs. Add [...] Include parsley and chives, and one of the **following:** dill, fennel, sorrel. Also add a knob of butter. Shape this mixture into [...]
For the **sauce,** mince some peeled shrimps and mix with lots of sour cream.
[...] As a main course, serve with boiled new potatoes and **broccoli;** as a starter, serve with crusty bread.

Getting it right

Washomatic for sale. This machine is a genuine bargain: it is only 12 years old; there is not a single visible patch of rust on it; last but not least, it does not leak. Phone Johnny on 324 5543.
Attention, old pen collectors: Green Silhouette pen for sale, 1952 model. Features **included:** original case, gold nib, embossed logo. Phone Pipa Pentop, 324 5682.
For sale or **hire:** garage in Bach Alley. Contact Mrs Lucas, 3 Bach Square.
Wanted: young person to deliver newspapers in Combe Park area. Must have own bike. Apply to Nat's News.
Gardener sought. The following qualifications are **required:** familiarity with Supermow, sound knowledge of organic vegetable growing and garden pest control. Phone 324 3344.

Hair excesses

Come to **us** for a wide range of hair care: perms, hair straightening, colour change, highlights, beading, hair extensions.
Our perms are perfect in every way: gentle, **lasting** and adapted to suit your face shape. Choose between three wonderful shampoos: frosted yogurt and banana for dry hair; lemon and lime cocktail for greasy hair; finally, for problem hair, mango and chilli revitalizing **magic** or Brazil nut balsam.
Always follow up a shampoo with a good conditioner: this guarantees good hair condition. Amongst our dozens of choices, we recommend **either** deep action strawberry, marigold petal extract or luxury oatmilk.

Treat yourself **to** a head massage, the ideal treatment for tired heads. You get a 15 minute massage given by an expert; generous amounts of the best head massage oils; a shampoo and blow dry.
We give you the hair shape you want. Once you have it, you will want to keep it; to help you, we stock 30 varieties of hair spray. Also in stock: hundreds of lacquers, hair **gels** and waxes.

Pages 44-45

Ask a straight question

Only number 1 is an indirect question: *I asked her if she could bring him to my party.* All the others need a question mark on the end.

Awkward questions

1   Do you live here?
2   Where were you at eleven o'clock last night?
3   What are the names of the four friends who were watching TV with you?
4   Did you or one of your friends hear anything unusual?
5   Do you have a friend called Jack?
6   Was he here last night?
7   Have you heard of the Burly Gang, a gang of thugs who hang around the neighbourhood?
8   Hasn't Jack ever mentioned them to you or boasted about being their leader?
9   Why did you lie when I asked you if you had heard anything unusual?
10 Was it you who gave Jack the key to your parents' garage so he could hide there last night?

Searching questions

One day, you'll leave, won't **you?**
When I asked you last summer,
You said you'd be true,
But now, I just **wonder.**
Why is it always me
That gets left **behind?**
In this state, I can't see
How life can ever be **kind.**

Friends are no **better.**
Why are they never around
When I need a **shoulder?**
Oh, when will I stop feeling so **blue?**

Questionnaire mix-up

2b), 3a), 4c), 5a), 6a), 7b), 8c), 9a), 10b).

Them books or *those books*? *You was* or you *were*? It is often difficult to know how to put your words together correctly, but this book will help you improve your

grammar skills. It contains fun puzzles that give you lots of practice, as well as simple explanations and guidelines to help you with tricky grammar points.

What is grammar?

Grammar is the way you use words and put them together into sentences that everyone can understand. The rules of grammar help you build sentences that make sense to other people. They tell you how to put words in the right order and use them correctly.

To use these rules properly, you need to know about the different types of word that make up our language.

Why is grammar important?

To make yourself properly understood, you need to know the rules about things like word order. Putting things in the wrong place can completely change the meaning of a sentence:

Ann ate the fish.

The fish ate Ann.

This book will help you avoid mistakes that could make people misunderstand what you are trying to say.

It will also help you improve your English. In everyday situations (when talking or writing to family or friends), people often say things that are not strictly correct. In formal situations, though, like interviews or exams, it is important to use your language correctly.

Besides, even little mistakes like getting one word wrong can change your meaning:

The owner of the car, which was enormous, polished it proudly.

The owner of the car, who was enormous, polished it proudly.

Using this book

On pages 67-71 you can find out about the different types of word that make up our language. Knowing about these will help you understand grammar and use it correctly.

On pages 72-90 there are simple explanations and guidelines to help you with tricky points that people often get wrong. For each double page, read the guidelines first, then test yourself with the puzzles. Try all of these, even ones that look easy. They may show up something you have not understood.

This is not a write-in book, so you will need paper and a pen or pencil to write your answers down. You can check your answers on pages 91-95.

Watch out for boxes like this one. They contain guidelines and tests on confusing pairs or groups of words that people often slip up on (such as *to* and *too*).

Changing grammar

English grammar is constantly changing. This is because new ways of saying things become accepted and tricky points that people find hard to follow get forgotten. This book does not deal with difficult areas that few people know about. It concentrates instead on common problems and mistakes that actually make what you write or say seem wrong.

In Britain and America, grammar has developed in different ways, so there are many small differences in the way British and American people speak English. For example: a British person might say, "Have you got a pen?" but an American would say, "Do you have a pen?"

Similarly, people from different parts of Britain often have different ways of saying things.

Here, and on the next four pages, you can learn the names for different types of word and find out about the jobs they do in a sentence. You can test what you have learned by doing the puzzles.

Nouns

A **noun** is a word which names a thing, a place, a person or an animal:

drum **Egypt**

A noun can be **singular** (when naming one thing, as in *cat*) or **plural** (when naming more than one, as in *cats*).

A noun often has a small introducing word called an **article** (*the*, *a* or *an*) in front. For example: _the_ sea, _a_ car. Nouns which are names of people (and many that are place names) do not have articles in front. For example: *Katie, France, New York.*

Adjectives

An **adjective** is a describing word. It tells you what a noun is like. For example, it can tell you what something looks like, or how big it is. Numbers can also be adjectives: they tell you how many things are being talked about. Here are some common adjectives: *red, large, excellent, ugly.*

Jumbled nouns

Can you complete this story by unscrambling the jumbled nouns? (Use the picture clues below to help you.)

Four criminals were arrested yesterday in **Pisar** after they tried to steal the Mona Lisa. Pretending to be **ranclees**, the thieves persuaded museum officials to let them remove the priceless **gnapinit**. However, as they were leaving the building, a **clamponie** recognized them as known villains, and the crooks dropped their loot and ran for it. The museum's revolving **rodos** proved to be more than they had bargained for, though. The doors jammed halfway round, and when a passing police **nav** stopped to investigate, **sodg** were able to surround the trapped villains. They are now firmly locked up in **rosnip**, and the famous picture is back in place ready for the weekend **russitot**.

Pisar ranclees gnapinit

clamponie rodos nav

sodg rosnip russitot

Give and take

Find four nouns and three adjectives in sentences 1 to 4. Then write out sentences A to D, completing them with the nouns and adjectives you have found.

1 **Bangkok is often very busy.**
2 **Sarah ran away screaming.**
3 **A black dog was barking loudly.**
4 **The rusty bicycle finally collapsed.**

A **They had bought the ... old car in ... .**
B **Where is ... today?**
C **Outside the house stood a shiny ... .**
D **I'm too ... to take the ... for a walk today.**

Verbs

A **verb** is an action word. It tells you what someone or something is doing. For example: *She is working*. Verbs can also show a state (*We live here, He is ill*).

Verbs are very important. They can turn a meaningless group of words (*lions deer*) into a proper sentence*: *Lions attack deer*.

A verb can also tell you about a past action (*They attacked*) or a future action (*They will attack*). There are different forms, or **tenses**, for talking about past, present and future actions. Verbs also change depending on who or what is doing the action (*I attack, He attacks*).

Subject and Object

The person or thing that does an action is called the **subject**. For example, in the sentence *Tim left the house*, *Tim* is the subject. In *He lives next door*, *He* is the subject.

The person or thing that is affected by the action is called the **object**. There are two kinds of object. A **direct object** is affected directly by an action (for example, *the letter* in the sentence *Matthew sent the letter*). An **indirect object** is usually the person or thing for whom or to whom an action is done. For example: *his sister* in *Matthew sent the letter to his sister*.

Pronouns

A **pronoun** is a word you use to replace a noun. Here are some common ones: *I, me, she, it, we, us, them, mine, his, yours*.

Pronouns make language less repetitive. For example, think of two sentences like these: *The frightened girl peered outside. She saw three*

men waiting below. Without the pronoun *she*, you would have to repeat *the frightened girl*, which would sound very clumsy.

To do the puzzles on these pages you may need to look back at some of the things that are explained on page 67.

Pronoun fillers

Some pronouns are missing from the report below. Read it through and then decide which pronoun each number stands for.

A yellow lesser-spotted, flat-billed frogcatcher, previously thought to be extinct, has been spotted in the Ice-pie National Park on the east coast. ..1.. was identified by keen birdwatcher, Caesar Lotterfeather. ..2.. said yesterday, "..3.. had been out spotting with a couple of friends, and as ..4.. were setting off home, ..1.. walked out right in front of us." Caesar said ..2.. and his friends were amazed to see the bird so near ..5.. .

"..3..'ve been coming here for twenty years but until now ..3..'ve only ever seen seagulls and the odd tern. ..4.. couldn't believe our eyes when we saw the frogcatcher cleaning its feet right in front of ..6.." Caesar was looking forward to reporting back to his wife. "..7.. is always telling ..8.. that ..3.. am wasting my time watching birds. Now ..3.. can really prove to ..9.. that my hobby's worthwhile."

*For more about sentences, see page 72.

——Identity parade——

In the list below there are five verbs, five nouns, and five words that can be either. Decide which group each word belongs to. Then fit the words that can be either verbs or nouns into sentences 1 to 5.

scream	follow	window
undo	study	hope
add	desk	wander
write	fly	shirt
climb	drawer	girl

1 My sister is hoping to ... law at university.
2 We managed to ... up onto the ridge of the mountain.
3 Her only ... now is that the train is running late.
4 When the man jumped out from behind the door, she let out a loud ... .
5 Mark swatted the ... that kept buzzing around the room.

——Sentence spinner——

Each ring of this circle contains a jumbled sentence. Rearrange the words in the rings so that each word is in the section labelled with its grammar name. You should be able to find five sentences by reading clockwise around the circle, starting with a pronoun each time.

Which sentence still makes sense when its object and subject are swapped over?

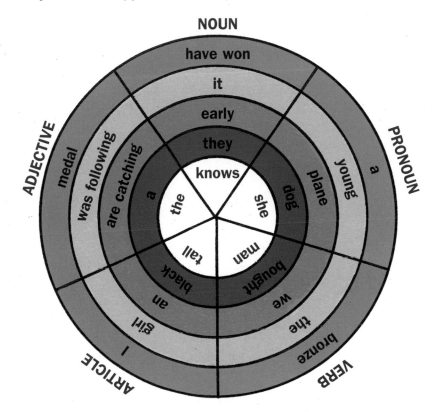

——A sack of words——

Arrange the words in this sack into five lists, putting all the nouns, verbs, adjectives, pronouns and articles together.

affect/effect

What is the difference between the words *affect* and *effect*? One is a verb and one is usually a noun, but which is which? Check by looking in a dictionary, then decide which one should go in each of the sentences below.

1 What is the ... of adding flour to water?
2 That film was really good. There were lots of special ...s.
3 I had a cold, but it didn't really ... me very badly.
4 Her illness had a very bad ... on her exam results.
5 The weather can ... the way you feel.

Adverbs

An **adverb** is like an adjective, but instead of describing a noun or a pronoun, it tells you more about a verb, an adjective, or even another adverb. An adverb describes how, when or where something happens.

Here are some examples using adverbs: *He smiled <u>politely</u>, Liz drives <u>slowly</u>, We arrived <u>late</u>, Jo lives <u>there</u>, I'm <u>only</u> joking.*

Conjunctions

A **conjunction** is a linking word. It joins other words and groups of words together. Without conjunctions, sentences sound short and jerky. For example: *He closed his eyes. He didn't fall asleep.* The conjunction *but* can turn these into a single sentence: *He closed his eyes, <u>but</u> he didn't fall asleep.*

Here are some common conjunctions: *and, but, or, yet, therefore, so, because, although, while.*

Prepositions

A **preposition** is a word that tells you how one thing is related to another. It is normally attached to a noun or a pronoun.

A lot of prepositions show where one thing is in relation to another. For example: *The dog is lying <u>on</u> the bed.*

Other prepositions show when something happens in relation to something else. For example: *Mike's parents are coming to stay <u>before</u> Christmas.*

Here are some common prepositions: *in, on, under, to, before, after, around, near, down, over, up, past, between, into.*

Lots of verbs look as if they are followed by prepositions (for example, *to break <u>down</u>, to cheer <u>up</u>, to break <u>in</u>*), but in fact, in these cases, these little words are thought of as part of the verb.

Doubling up

Some words can do one job in one sentence, and a different one elsewhere. So, depending on the job they are doing, they can belong to different groups of words. Here are some examples:

1 *Her* and words like *this* and *that* can be pronouns (*Look at <u>her</u>; <u>That</u>'s a pity*) and also adjectives (*It is <u>her</u> jacket; Look at <u>that</u> coat*).

2 Some words, like *hard, late* and *fast*, can be adverbs (*They ran <u>fast</u>; The train arrived <u>late</u>*) or adjectives (*Andy is a <u>fast</u> runner; We are getting a <u>late</u> train*).

3 Words like *so* and *however* can be conjunctions (*He wasn't in, <u>so</u> I left; I am fine, <u>however</u> Jane is not very well*) or adverbs (*I am <u>so</u> tired; <u>However</u> hard he works, he won't pass his exams now*).

——Scrambled——

Unjumble the prepositions below, then decide which one fits each sentence:

trafe **enetweb** **scarso** **toni** **drune**

1. My car was parked ... the truck and the motorbike.
2. They walked home ... the party.
3. The dog jumped ... the lake.
4. The prisoner ran as fast as he could ... the bridge.
5. The money was hidden ... the bed.

Sentence building

Put these parts of sentences together into the most likely pairs, joining each pair with one of the conjunctions shown in blue.

He couldn't remember her name,

she was jogging.

He forced the door open

crept quietly into the house.

it had already gone.

Michelle rushed to the window and looked for the car,

he had met her before.

my knee hurts.

I can't play tennis today

She listened to music on her headphones

| while | because | but | and | although |

Sentence parts

The sentences below have been split into parts. Write them out, circling each part in the right colour to show which grammar group it belongs to.

noun (subject)	article
noun (object)	verb
pronoun(subject)	adverb
pronoun (object)	conjunction
adjective	preposition

1 The / dog / ran / into / the / road / and / the / car / just / missed / it.
2 We / are having / a / big / party, / so / you / must come.
3 The / big / bear / escaped / from / the / zoo / and / was / never / seen / again.
4 The / dancers / were / so / shocked / they / had to stop / the / show.

borrow/lend   teach/learn

People often confuse these words. Borrowing is when you take something from someone for a while, but lending is when you give something for a while.

Teaching means showing someone how to do something, or telling them about it. Learning means finding out.

Decide which verb (*borrow*, *lend*, *teach* or *learn*) fits each speech bubble.

Did you ... my shoes again last night?

He is going to ... to speak Spanish before he goes.

Can anyone ... me some money?

She is trying to ... me to sing.

Fill the gap

Choose the correct adjectives or adverbs from the lists below to fill in the gaps in this story. (Use each once only.)

As Ian stepped into the house and wiped his ..1.. shoes on the mat, he heard a ..2.. crash from upstairs. He closed the door ..3.. and waited, trembling. There was no sound. Ian crept across the ..4.. hallway, his heart pounding ..5.. . He tiptoed up the ..6.. stairs, moving ..7.. from one to the next. On the landing, he paused and held his breath. He could just hear a ..8.. sound coming from the sitting room. Ian breathed in ..9.., rested his trembling hand on the door and then ..10.. flung it open. As ..11.. faces appeared all around the room, the lights went on, and a chorus of familiar voices cried ..12.., "Happy Birthday!" Ian sank ..13.. into a chair.

Adjectives: cheerful, loud, muddy, empty, creaky, faint

Adverbs: merrily, thankfully, quietly, deeply, heavily, lightly, suddenly

71

A sentence is a group of words that makes sense on its own. Most sentences have a subject and a verb. For example: *The cat ran across the garden.* Short exclamations, questions and greetings are also sentences, even though they have no subject or verb. For example: *How amazing! What? Good morning.* A sentence always starts with a capital letter and ends with a full stop (.), question mark (?) or exclamation mark (!).

Clauses and phrases

Sentences can be made up of **clauses** (groups of words that contain verbs) and **phrases** (groups of words without verbs).

| A phrase adds extra meaning to a sentence. | A main clause makes sense on its own. |

In a panic, she ripped up the letter that he had written.

A subordinate clause depends on a main clause for its meaning. It is usually introduced by a word like *who, which, that, when, where, because, if, although, while* or *before.* Often, though, *who, which* and *that* can be missed out: *In a panic, she ripped up the letter he had written.**

Sentence building

Sentences come in all shapes and sizes. They can be:

a) **simple**, with only one subject. For example: *The girl wrote a story.*

b) simple, but with adjectives, adverbs and phrases added: *The little girl quickly wrote a funny story about a seahorse.*

c) **compound****, with subordinate clauses and extra main clauses: *The little girl took out her pen, and quickly wrote a funny story about a seahorse which swam across the Atlantic and then drowned in a puddle.*

Keep your sentences short, so that they are absolutely clear. Long, complicated sentences can sound clumsy.

Sentence-splitting

The two articles below are each made up of one long, clumsy sentence. Break them both into two by taking out a comma and a conjunction and adding a full stop and a capital letter.

The **Lengthy Express**

BAGGED

Longville mayoress Mrs. Ponsonby-Smythe was in high spirits on Saturday, as she opened the church fête which Longville has been organizing for the past three weeks, but she refused to comment on the incident last week in which local woman Cora Redhanded attacked her with a handbag, accusing her of stealing a bag of flour from her grocery store.

COUCH POTATO KIDS

Children are much less healthy these days, because they spend so much time sitting like couch potatoes in front of the television, or playing computer games while they stuff their faces with crisps and fizzy drinks, and they don't get much exercise either, because they go everywhere by car or by public transport, instead of walking.

*There is more about this on page 82.
**The word "compound" means "made up of several parts".

Clause-spotting

Decide whether each group of words below is a main clause, a subordinate clause or a phrase. Put one of each type together to make four sentences, then arrange these into a short story, beginning *In the house next door ...*

In the house next door

in a fast car

which had incredibly long legs.

in a panic

One day he let it out

which squashed the poor stick insect.

while Mrs. Kettani was in her garden.

because she was terrified of large insects.

They arrived

She phoned the police

my friend kept a stick insect

in the street

Sentence stretch

Add an adjective, an adverb and a subordinate clause from the lists below to each of these sentences. (Put the adverb just in front of the verb, and the subordinate clause at the end.)

1 The monkey ate six bananas.

2 She eats at the restaurant.

3 He drove the car into a ditch.

4 Joanna walked up to the horse.

Adjectives: hungry, young, new, Chinese.

Adverbs: stupidly, slowly, greedily, often.

Subordinate clauses:
where her brother is a waiter.
which had thrown her off its back.
when the zookeeper had gone.
because he was fiddling with the radio.

an/a

an usually goes in front of:

a) words that begin with a vowel (*a, e, i, o* or *u*)
   egg, apple

b) words beginning with a letter such as *h* when it sounds like a vowel
   hour, heir

c) single letters (often in sets of initials) that sound like vowels
   SOS (*S* is said as "ess")
   MP (*M* is said as "em")

a usually goes in front of:

a) words that begin with a consonant (a letter that is not a vowel)
   door, book, clock

b) words beginning with vowels that sound like consonants
   university, European (both begin with "yuh" sounds)
   one-way street begins with a "wuh" sound)

Add either *an* or *a* to each of these nine sentences:

1 He gave me ... used railway ticket.

2 Jill said she had seen ... UFO.

3 They gave her ... X-ray and said she'd be fine.

4 From his window he has ... incredible view over New York.

5 This is ... one-way street.

6 Sometimes, a friend can turn into ... enemy.

7 It was such ... hot day.

8 It was ... honest answer.

9 He has ... older brother.

73

On these two pages you can find some useful hints on how to arrange words so that your sentences are as clear as possible.

Keeping together

Words that are connected to each other should always be kept together in a sentence. Here are two rules to help you with this:

1 Try to keep the subject and the verb as close together as possible, especially in long sentences. For example: *Jim read the letter one last time, while Emma went to the phone and called the police.*

The meaning can be unclear if the subject and the verb are far apart: *Jim, while Emma went to the phone and called the police, read the letter one last time.*

2 Phrases and subordinate clauses should go as near as possible to the words they refer to.

If you put them in the wrong place, your sentence may sound very strange. For example: *The farmer rounded up the sheep that had run away with the sheepdog's help.*

Moving the phrase *with the sheepdog's help* nearer to *the farmer* makes the meaning clear: *With the sheepdog's help, the farmer rounded up the sheep that had run away.*

Shifting adverbs

Certain adverbs, like *only* and *just*, give sentences a slightly different meaning, depending on their position. You should normally put them in front of what they refer to, as shown here:

I told only Christopher that I had won second prize. (Christopher was the only person I told.)

I only told Christopher that I had won second prize. (It was the only thing I told him.)

I told Christopher that I had only won second prize. (I told him I had only won second prize, not first.)

Split infinitives

The **infinitive** of a verb (*to* plus the verb, as in *to go, to work, to drive*) is its most basic form. You should not break up (or split) the two parts of the infinitive. This means it is wrong to use phrases such as *to boldly go*. You should either put *boldly* in front of or after *to go*.

—————— **Splitting up** ——————

Sarah's family are going away for the week. Spot the split infinitives in the notes they have left, then move the words that are splitting them to the end of the sentences.

You can finish all the food in the freezer, except for the chocolate cake I made for Dad's birthday, and the leg of lamb, which I'd like you to please take out on Saturday. Also, before Mr. Hopkins drops by on Wednesday, I'd like you to thoroughly hoover the sitting room.

Before you go out, remember to carefully double-lock the door.

Please don't forget to put Bingo out before you go to bed. You need to every night feed my goldfish.

Could you remember to regularly water the tomatoes? By the way, I told Mary you'd try to quickly drop in on her.

SEE YOU ON SATURDAY – WE'RE GOING TO IF POSSIBLE TRY TO GET THE AFTERNOON TRAIN. PERHAPS YOU COULD PICK US UP FROM THE STATION IF WE GIVE YOU A RING?

Picture puzzlers

Next to each pair of pictures below, there is a short sentence, and one phrase or clause (in yellow). Make two new sentences (one to match each picture) by inserting this phrase or clause in two different places in the sentence*.

1 **The girl gave the envelope to the man.**
with the dog

2 **The man beat his rival.**
who was wearing blue

3 **The plant was in the corner of the room.**
with the yellow flowers

4 **Jane rested her foot on the top rung of the ladder.**
which was shaking

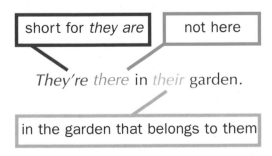

Adverb adding

Write out sentence 1 three times, putting the adverb *just* in a different place each time, so that the sentences have the meanings given in A, B and C.

Then do the same with sentence 2, using the adverb *only*.

Sentence 1: He's told me I will have to take it easy for a few days.
A **He told me a minute ago.**
B **The only thing I have to do is take it easy.**
C **I have to take it easy, but only for a few days.**

Sentence 2: There were a few chocolates left, but Sue ate two.
A **There weren't many chocolates, but Sue took two anyway.**
B **There were some chocolates left, but Sue only took two.**
C **There were some chocolates left, but Sue was the only person who took two.**

their/they're/there

Because they sound the same, it is easy to get *their, they're* and *there* mixed up. Here you can see the different meanings of these words:

| short for *they are* | not here |

| in the garden that belongs to them |

They're there in their garden.

There is also used with *to be* to say things like *there is* (or *there's*) and *there are*.

For sentences 1 to 6, which word or group of words in brackets fits the gap?

1 **There ... in a netball team.**
(daughter is/all/are seven people)
2 **Their ... outside.**
(are two men/dog is/waiting)
3 **They're ... in the swimming pool.**
(still/dog is/we were)
4 **Their ... way.**
(lawyer is on his/is a tree in the/on their)
5 **Isn't she there ...?**
(new teacher/any more)
6 **They're ... on holiday.**
(friend is/were two of us/away)

75

*You may need to add commas to make the meaning clear. See page 82.

Simple agreements

Always make sure that the subject agrees with (matches) the verb. Here you can see what this means:

| singular subject | verb must be singular |

Sarah is out,
but *the twins are* upstairs.

| plural subject | verb must be plural |

Tricky cases

Sometimes it is difficult to know whether to use a singular or plural verb with the subject. Here are some hints to help you:

1 The words *anyone, everyone, no one* and *each* are always followed by a singular verb. For example: *Everyone is asleep.*

The words *many, both, (a) few* and *several* are always followed by a plural verb. For example: *Several are missing.*

2 When the subject is two words joined by *and* (as in *Annie and her friend*), you use a plural verb: *Here come Annie and her friend.*

3 When the subject is a group of words, such as *members of the gang*, the verb must agree with the actual word it relates to:

*These **members** of the gang are the toughest.*

| verb relates to this word (the *members* are the toughest, not the *gang*) | verb is plural to match *members* |

4 Singular words which name groups of people (like *family, team* or *school*) can be used with either singular or plural verbs.

To talk about the group as a whole, you normally use a singular verb: *Each team has three turns.* To talk about it as a group of members, you can use a plural verb: *The team were excited about the match.*

── Island mission ──

Agent Craxitall is on the trail of the notorious criminal, Ivor Cunningplan. He has discovered some pieces of the torn-up instructions for Ivor's latest mission. Fit them together to find out what Ivor has to do and where he is heading.

FIVE MEMBERS OF THE GANG

IF SOMEONE SAYS: "HERE COMES

KNOWS THAT THE DOCUMENTS ARE BEING DELIVERED BY A MAN WITH A LIMP.

LIE IN THE WYLIN OCEAN.

TRACKHAM DOWN DETECTIVES

CODE NAME: CRAXITALL AGENT 008

TO THE LEADER OF THE SNEAK STREET GANG.

YOUR MISSION IS TO DELIVER THE SILICON DOCUMENTS

FIRST GO TO THE ISLANDS OF SKEE-MING, WHICH

THEN HEAD FOR THE CITY OF SKA-LEE-WAGS, WHICH

ONCE THERE, YOU WILL EASILY LOCATE SNEAK STREET. ON FRIDAY NIGHT,

EACH MEMBER

ART FULFOX AND HIS DOG," THEN IT IS NOT SAFE TO DELIVER THE DOCUMENTS.

ARE MEETING ON THE CORNER OF SNEAK STREET.

WALK UP TO THE GANG. IF SOMEONE SAYS: "HERE COME

IS ON THE NORTHERNMOST ISLAND.

ART FULFOX," YOU CAN DROP THEM OFF AND RETURN TO HQ.

Beach breaks

In this game, each white space shows the first half of a sentence. Starting at the blue arrow, move around from space to space, following the direction of the footprint containing the matching half sentence. You must go through all the white spaces before taking a red exit. Which exit, A to G, will you take?

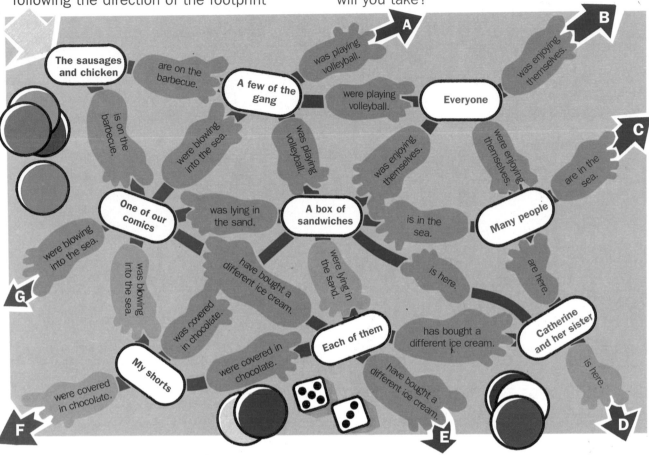

The sausages and chicken — are on the barbecue.
is on the barbecue.
A few of the gang — was playing volleyball.
were playing volleyball.
was playing volleyball.
were blowing into the sea.
Everyone — was enjoying themselves.
were enjoying themselves.
One of our comics — was lying in the sand.
A box of sandwiches — is in the sea.
Many people — are in the sea.
were blowing into the sea.
was blowing into the sea.
have bought a different ice cream.
were lying in the sand.
is here.
are here.
Each of them — has bought a different ice cream.
Catherine and her sister — is here.
was covered in chocolate.
My shorts — were covered in chocolate.
were covered in chocolate.
have bought a different ice cream.

off/of

Off is nearly always connected to a verb. It can be a preposition (*They dropped it off the bridge*) or part of a verb (*They got off at the bus stop*).

Of is normally used after adjectives (as in *afraid of*), or after words that show quantity or numbers of things (as in *a few of, some of, a piece of, lots of*).

Of is sometimes used with a verb. In these cases, it often means *about* (for example, *to dream of, to think of*).

Which of these sentences is missing *off*, and which is missing *of*?

1 He is very proud ... his polar bear costume.
2 Kathy stopped ... in Zambia on her way to Swaziland.
3 Her brother reminds me ... a chimpanzee.
4 Most ... the chocolate fudge cake had already been eaten.
5 As she was getting ... the train, she saw the man.
6 Vicky has always been terrified ... cats.
7 The plane took ... late.

Fill the gaps

Fit one of the yellow words below into each sentence.

1 There ... layers of dust on the piano.
2 "Here ... Ann and Graham!" she shrieked, pointing across the street.
3 A little bit of money ... a long way.
4 When we got back, there ... a bucketful of tomatoes on the doorstep.
5 Most motorbikes are cheaper than cars and ... much faster.
6 Success ... more important to him than happiness.

is was go were are goes

Verbs have different forms for talking about the past, the present and the future. For example:

I worked, *I am working*, *I will work*. These different verb forms are called **tenses**.

Tenses

Here you can see the main tenses. The examples, using the verb *to wait*, show how they are formed for most verbs.

	PAST		PRESENT	FUTURE
past perfect	past simple*	present perfect	present simple*	future
had waited	*waited*	*have/has waited*	*wait/waits*	*shall/will wait*

For many common verbs, the past tenses are irregular (not formed in the way shown here). There is a list of common irregular verbs on page 16.

Many of these tenses also have **continuous** forms, such as the present continuous (*I am waiting*), and past continuous (*I was waiting*). These are normally used for something that is, was or will already be happening at a particular time.

There are other ways of talking about the future. For example, to talk about plans or things you intend to do, you can use *going to* with the verb (as in *Tomorrow I am going to write to my parents*).

Showing order

To talk about several things that happened at different times, you show the order they happened in by using different tenses. For example, when you use the past simple to talk about things that happened in the past, you can use the past perfect to show an action that took place even further back in time:

happened second

happened first (a while ago)

He *walked up* to the man who *had won*, and as he *handed* him the gleaming gold medal, he *said*, "Soon you *will be* famous."

both happened third (just after what happened second)

will happen fourth

When talking about a set of events, be careful not to jump from one tense to another (unless you are talking about things that happened at different times). Look at the example below.

She rushed downstairs, opened the door and picks up the parcel which the postman had delivered.

This should say *picked*.

like/as

You use *like* and *as* to compare things. Like goes in front of a noun or a pronoun. For example: *She is like her father.*

As goes in front of a clause (which has a subject and a verb). For example: *Everything was just as he had left it.*

As is also used in many other expressions which compare things in some way: *as if*, *as good as*, *as usual*, *as before*.

Make six sentences by joining a first half (on the left) with a second half (on the right), using *like*, *as* or *as if*.

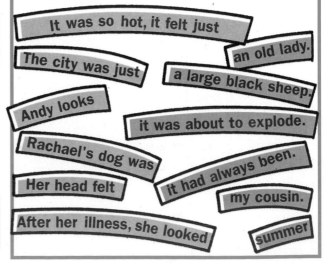

It was so hot, it felt just

an old lady.

The city was just

a large black sheep.

Andy looks

it was about to explode.

Rachael's dog was

it had always been.

Her head felt

my cousin.

After her illness, she looked

summer

*In negative sentences (ones that use *not*) and in questions, use *did* with the past simple (*Did I wait?*) and *do/does* with the present simple (*He does not wait*).

Tense trippers

Louise has kept a diary of the cycling trip she went on with some friends, but she has put twelve verbs in the wrong tense. Can you correct her mistakes?

Monday

Just before lunch Stuart got a puncture. No one had a puncture repair kit, so we have to walk miles to the nearest town. When we finally got there, someone directed us to a bike shop, so we go all the way there and then find it was closed.

Tuesday

The day went well until we get caught behind a herd of sheep on a narrow lane. It took us two hours to get past them, so by the time we got to the youth hostel, it's completely full.

Wednesday

Stopped for lunch in a little village. Left our bikes by the church, went to a café, and when we come out, Sheila's bike has disappeared. Then suddenly we spotted the local vicar riding the missing bike, so we flag him down and he explained everything. The poor vicar sold his own bike a year ago, but he keeps forgetting, so every time he sees a black bike he thought it's his.

Thursday

Arrived at the station to get the train home. We loaded our bikes on board and then go for a coffee while we are waiting. Suddenly, Stuart noticed that the train was leaving! We put our bikes on the wrong one!

Which is which?

Copy the list of verbs below. Then decide which tenses they are in, and underline each one as shown here:

past perfect
past simple
present perfect
present simple
future

have crashed
smiled
had promised
sit
had visited
will understand
did not arrive
buys
has spotted
will drive
invaded
sing
had painted

Getting snappy

Louise wanted to arrange her photos in the order in which they were taken, but she has muddled them up.

For each caption (A, B, C and D), write out the numbers of the photos in the order she should arrange them.

A **At a local market, we met the boy who had fixed Stuart's bike, so we all went to the funfair together.**

B **Every morning, fishermen in this village sell fresh fish that they have caught from their boats. By lunchtime, they will have none left.**

C **After we'd spotted the vicar riding the bike Sheila had left outside the church, we all went for a coffee together.**

D **On Tuesday, we had a picnic, and then went for a swim in a little cove we'd read about the night before.**

Hints

These hints will help you decide which tenses to use in long sentences:

1 When the verb in the main clause is in the past tense (as in *I was cross*), the verbs in the subordinate clauses usually go into a past tense as well (*I was cross because he had not locked the door*).

2 When the verb in the main clause is in the future (*We will go*), or has a future meaning, verbs in the subordinate clauses usually go in to the present (*We will go when he arrives*).

Which past tense?

You use the **past simple** to talk about something that happened at a particular time (as in *She arrived yesterday*).

You use the **present perfect** when it is not important to know exactly when something happened (*I have been to Egypt*), or when something is still going on (*I have lived here for two years*).

The present perfect is made using *has* or *have* and the **past participle**. For most verbs, the past participle is exactly like the past simple (*I called, I have called*).

The past participle is also used with *had* to form the **past perfect** (*I had called*). There is more about forming tenses on page 78.

Irregulars

Some common verbs have past simples and past participles that are **irregular**. This means they are not formed in the usual way (by adding *ed*). Here you can see a few tricky ones:

verb	past simple	past participle
to be	was/were*	been
to begin	began	begun
to break	broke	broken
to do	did	done
to drink	drank	drunk
to eat	ate	eaten
to forget	forgot	forgotten
to give	gave	given
to go	went	gone/been**
to run	ran	run
to sing	sang	sung
to swim	swam	swum
to take	took	taken

> **Can you think of any more verbs that have irregular past simples or past participles? You will need to know some others to do all the puzzles on these pages.**

─────────**Lost for words**─────────

Which word from the yellow list below fits which speech bubble?

I have ... too much ice cream.

I ... a lot of ice cream when I was in Italy.

I have just ... my sister's sunglasses.

Last week I ... Mr. Bailey's window.

I ... in the bath this morning.

I have just ... across the lake.

I ... across it yesterday.

I have ... all my homework.

Nicky ... hers last week.

broke/broken/ swum/swam/ eaten/ate/ sang/done/did

80   *Use *was* with *I, he, she* and *it,* and *were* with *you, we* and *they.*
     **Use *gone* when the subject is still away, and *been* when they have already returned.

Andrew's desk

Picture A shows what was on Andrew's desk one morning, and picture B shows what was there in the evening. Choosing verbs from the list below, write four sentences (beginning each one *He has ...*) to show what Andrew has done at his desk during the day.

Then rewrite these sentences, using the past simple. Begin each one *In the afternoon, ...*

to blow out, to break, to eat, to write

Tense trouble

Spot which verb is in the wrong tense in each of the sentences below.

1 **They will have to tidy up the house before their parents will get back.**
2 **Oliver had just finished writing when the examiner tells them to put down their pens.**
3 **Lots of people visit the exhibition when it opens next month.**
4 **I was furious because the train has been late.**
5 **She has been to Hong Kong last year.**
6 **They lived in New York for six years, and have no plans to move away.**

can/may/might

Here you can see when to use *can*, *may* and *might*:

	can	*may*	*might*
1 Talking about something that is possible	use *can* to talk about something that you are able to do: *I can swim.*	use *may* for something that is possible and quite likely: *I may go for a swim.*	use *might* for something that is possible but not so likely. *I might go for a swim.*
2 Asking for permission	To ask permission or to give it, you can use *can* or *may. May* is more grammatically correct though, so you should use it in formal situations: *May I go home?* or *You may leave.* Use *can* in less formal situations: *Can I have a biro?* or *You can have two chocolates.*		*might* is sometimes used in very formal situations: *Might I ask a question?*
3 Giving permission			never use *might*

Decide which word, *may*, *might* or *can* should fill the gaps in these sentences:

1 **I am very glad that Jenny ... speak French.**
2 **You ... spend as much money as you like.**
3 **... I borrow a pencil?** (talking to a friend)
4 **... I phone my parents?** (talking to someone you don't know)
5 **I ... go and see a film this afternoon, if it carries on raining.**

81

Could is often used instead of can to ask for permission. It is less direct (and more polite) than can.

Which, that, who, whom and *whose* are called **relative pronouns**. They usually introduce clauses which tell you more about a noun. For example: There are those *awful people who live at number 6.*

Different clauses

Relative pronouns work in different ways, depending on whether they are introducing an identifying or a non-identifying clause.

An **identifying clause** spells out who or what the noun is, as in *There is the dog which bit my rabbit.*

A **non-identifying clause** simply tells you more about a noun whose identity is already clear. Think of it as the part of the sentence that could go in brackets. For example: *Mr. Parker's dog, which bit my rabbit, has just attacked the milkman.*

When speaking, you do not often use non-identifying clauses. They are always split off from the rest of the sentence by commas, but identifying clauses are not.

Relative pronouns

Here you can see which relative pronoun to use, depending on whether you are talking about a person or a thing*:

IDENTIFYING CLAUSES

for people	who (or whom)/that
for things	which/that

1 *That* can often replace *who* or *which* (as in the man that stole the bananas).
2 You can often leave out the relative pronoun altogether: *That is the dog (which) I rescued.*

NON-IDENTIFYING CLAUSES

for people	who (or whom)
for things	which

1 You cannot use *that* instead of *who* or *which*.
2 You cannot leave out the relative pronoun.

Whom, whose

Whom can stand for a person, if that person is the object** of the clause (as in *That is the doctor whom I saw*). In spoken English, it is normally replaced with *who* or *that*.

Whose stands for someone to whom something belongs (*The man whose car I had hit chased me*).

Prepositions

After a preposition (see page 70), you use *whom* instead of *who*, and *which* instead of *that*. For example: *the man to whom I gave my ticket.* It is often easier, though, to turn the clause around and leave out the relative pronoun: *the man I gave my ticket to.*

Identity crisis

Rewrite the sentences below, removing any non-identifying clauses.

1 The fridge is full of bacon, which I eat every day.
2 The ring which he gave me was far too big.
3 The policeman who drove them home was very friendly.
4 My brother, who is a vet, is getting married.
5 The boat, which was found by a diver, had been underwater for thirty years.

Who or *whom*?

Write out these sentences, completing two with *who* and two with *whom*.

1 The friend with ... I went to Egypt has sent me a letter.
2 The people ... took the other path got there first.
3 Valerie, ... has just come back from Mexico, speaks fluent Spanish.
4 This is Jo, ... I met on the bus.

82 *For an animal, depending on how you think of it, you can either follow the pattern for people or for things.
**Remember, the subject does the action and the object has the action done to it.

Murder at Snoot Towers

Read this report on the murder of Lord Snoot, and decide which relative pronoun (below) should go in each space. Then use the plan of Snoot Towers to identify the most likely murderer.

Lord Snoot's body, ..1.. was found in the conservatory, was identified by his widow. Lady Snoot, ..2.. will inherit several million pounds from her husband, was in the drawing room with the gardener at the time of the murder, looking at designs for a sunken garden ..3.. she wanted putting in. Hugo Batty, ..4.. knew the truth about Snoot's business affairs, and to ..5.. Snoot had just given six thousand pounds, was working in the library. Will Snoot, ..6.. fiancée was lunching with his sister in the dining room (both women are eliminated from the inquiry), was shooting grouse in Snoot Forest. Lord Snoot had earlier forbidden him to marry his fiancée. The cook and the butler were in the pantry, ..7.. can only be reached from the drawing room. They said they heard Lord Snoot's cousin, Earl Toffeenose, talking in the billiard room with the nanny, ..8.. Snoot had just fired. Nobody passed through any of the rooms ..9.. anyone else was in around the time of the murder.

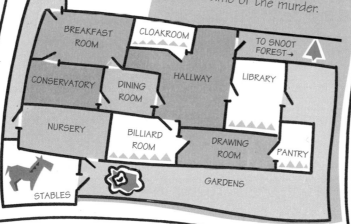

that/which
whom
who
which
whose
which
whom/that
that
who

BREAKFAST ROOM · CLOAKROOM · TO SNOOT FOREST→
CONSERVATORY · DINING ROOM · HALLWAY · LIBRARY
NURSERY · BILLIARD ROOM · DRAWING ROOM · PANTRY
STABLES · GARDENS

of 've

In speech, *have* is often shortened to *'ve* after *should, would, may, must, might* and so on. For example: *You should've gone.**

Be careful not to confuse *'ve* with *of*, which sounds very similar. Never use *of* instead of *have* with the words listed above.

Complete these pieces of conversation with *should've, would've, could've* and *must've*. (Use each once only.)

1 "She ... decided not to take her car, because I saw it parked in our street this morning."
2 "You really ... gone to the party: it was great fun."
3 "We ... driven a bit faster, but not much, as the roads are very wet."
4 "If it hadn't been raining, I ... come."

Who's who and what's what?

Look at the pictures, then decide which clause from the list on the right fits which sentence best. (Use each once only.)

1 The girl ... is near the boat.
2 The dog ... has black paws.
3 The ice cream ... is chocolate and vanilla.
4 The boy ... has red hair.
5 The cow ... has black ears.
6 The dog ... is near the boat.
7 The baby ... has a pink hat.
8 The man ... has a red sweater.

THE POLICEMAN IS CHASING
WHICH IS SWIMMING
WHICH THE BOY IS HOLDING
WHICH IS RUNNING
WHO IS SWIMMING
WHOM THE POLICEMAN IS CHASING
WHO IS RUNNING
THE WOMAN IS HOLDING

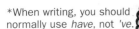

*When writing, you should normally use *have*, not *'ve*.

Comparatives and superlatives

Comparatives and superlatives are special forms of adjective that are used for comparing things.

You use a **comparative** (such as *taller, more intelligent*) to compare people or things with each other. For example: *Simon is <u>taller</u> than Andrew and Tim.*

You use a **superlative** (such as *the tallest, the most intelligent*) to show that one thing stands out above all the rest. For example: *Simon is <u>the tallest</u> in the class.*

Different forms

Most comparatives are made either by adding *er* to the adjective, or putting *more* in front of it. Most superlatives are made by adding *est* or putting *the most* in front.

The form you use depends on how many syllables the adjective has. A **syllable** is part of a word that contains a vowel sound. For example, *lazy* has two syllables containing the vowel sounds "ay" and "ee".

Here are some general rules on which form to use. Examples are shown in blue:

ADJECTIVE	COMPARATIVE	SUPERLATIVE
one-syllable adjective* *hard*	*-er* *harder*	*the -est* *the hardest*
one-syllable adjective ending in *e* *white*	*-r* *whiter*	*the -st* *the whitest*
adjective with two or more syllables *careful*	*more ...* *more careful*	*the most ...* *the most careful*
two-syllable adjective ending in *y* *funny*	*-er* (and change *y* to *i*) *funnier*	*the -est* (and change *y* to *i*) *the funniest*

The important thing to remember is that you either add *er* (or *est*) OR use *more* (or *the most*). Never do both.

Irregulars Here are some common adjectives which have irregular comparatives and superlatives:

ADJECTIVE	COMPARATIVE	SUPERLATIVE
good	*better*	*the best*
bad	*worse*	*the worst*
much/many	*more*	*the most*
little	*less*	*the least*

Adverbs, I/me

Adverbs also have comparative and superlative forms. These work just as for adjectives, except that for most long adverbs ending in y, you use *more/the most* instead of adding *er/est*.

It is common to use *me*, *him, her, us* and *them* after a comparative with *than* (as in *He is older than me*). In formal situations, though, people sometimes use *I, he, she, we* and *they* (*He is older than I*).

—Comparing climates—

Look at these charts of the temperature and total rainfall for two cities through the year. Then write out the sentences below, adding comparatives of *hot*, *cold* (for 1 and 2), *wet* and *dry* (for 3 and 4).

1 **In August, Weatherchester is ... than Seasonbury.**
2 **In January, Weatherchester is ... than Seasonbury.**
3 **In March, Seasonbury is ... than Weatherchester.**
4 **In September, Seasonbury is ... than Weatherchester.**

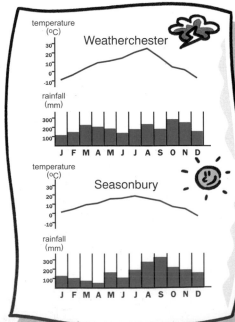

*For adjectives ending in *y* (such as *dry*), you change *y* to *i* (*drier, the driest*). For those ending in one vowel and one consonant (such as *hot*), you double the consonant (*hotter, the hottest*).

Character questionnaire

Jon and Tessa have done a magazine quiz, each of them putting their initial by the answer they have chosen. Based on their answers, and making comparatives from the adjectives on the list, write six sentences comparing Jon and Tessa. For example: *Jon is taller than Tessa.*

Quiz

NOSY
SELFISH
LAZY
FRIENDLY
PATIENT
CAREFUL

1 You have been waiting for a bus for half an hour. You:

a) wait patiently, feeling glad you are not in a hurry. J

b) pace up and down, looking at your watch. T

c) decide to walk – the exercise will do you good.

2 Arriving home, you realize you have forgotten to post an urgent letter for your mother. You:

a) pretend to have forgotten all about it until it is too late. J

b) ask your brother to post it on his way to football practice.

c) go straight out to post it before you forget again. T

3 There is a new girl in your class, and at lunchtime you notice her sitting on her own. You:

a) ask her to come and join you and your mates. T

b) make a point of talking to her later on.

c) ignore her. J

4 You are walking a friend's dog in the countryside. You:

a) put it on the lead every time you see a road ahead. J

b) keep an eye on it whenever you are on a road.

c) let it wander ahead – after all, the roads are very quiet. T

5 You hear your sister on the phone and she is clearly upset. You:

a) strain your ears to listen in. T

b) hum loudly, so you can't hear anything. J

c) listen in, then ask her later on what was wrong.

6 For your birthday you are given a small box of chocolates. You:

a) guzzle them in your room rather than share them around. J

b) offer them around once, then eat the rest yourself.

c) offer them to all your mates, leaving none for yourself. T

quite/quiet

People often confuse these words. *Quite* is an adverb that either means "fairly" (as in *I'm quite tired*), or "completely" (*I'm quite lost*). *Quiet* is an adjective that means the opposite of "noisy"/"loud".

Passed and *past* are also confusing. *Passed* can only be used as a verb (as in *He passed the salt*). *Past* can be used as an adjective (*the past year*), a noun (*He lives in the past*), a preposition (*She ran past me*) or an adverb (*A gull flew past*).

Write these sentences out, adding *quite, quiet, passed* or *past.*

1 You look ... washed out.
2 As Stefan walked ..., he noticed the man's gun.
3 It is very ... without Diane and Vicky.
4 Veronica was so happy when she ... her exams.
5 In the ... week, I have lost two umbrellas.
6 I have always found maths ... hard.

Moped mania

Sally is not sure which moped to buy. Using the table on the right, and the adjectives *wide, long, expensive, fast* and *heavy,* write five sentences to compare the Superwhizz and the Pipsqueak.

Then do the same for the Stumbly and the Featherzoom, and for the Pipsqueak and the Thriftyshift.

Sally can only spend £2000, and her garage is 0.5 x 2 metres. Which is the fastest moped she can buy?

Moped	Width (metres)	Length (metres)	Price (£)	Top speed (miles per hour)	Weight (kilos)
Superwhizz	0.5	1.9	2500	65	592
Pipsqueak	0.3	1.5	1800	50	520
Stumbly	0.6	1.9	1500	40	565
Featherzoom	0.5	2.1	1700	60	495
Thriftyshift	0.4	2	950	45	510

Conditional sentences are used to talk about things that can only happen under certain conditions*. For example: *If he said he was sorry, I would forgive him.*

There are three main types. They are made up of two clauses, each in a different tense, one of which is introduced by *if*. Most contain a verb in the **conditional** (such as *would go*) or **conditional perfect** (*would have gone*).

Type 1

if clause in present tense	other clause in future tense

"If I win an Olympic medal,
I will give all the prize money to charity."

This type is used to talk about something that is likely to happen. In the example, the person speaking has a good chance of winning an Olympic medal.

Type 2

if clause in past tense	other clause in conditional

"If I won an Olympic medal,
I would give all the prize money to charity."

This type is used to talk about something that is unlikely to happen. In the example, the person speaking is just imagining what it would be like to win an Olympic medal.

Type 3

if clause in past perfect	other clause in conditional perfect

"If I had won an Olympic medal,
I would have given all the prize money to charity."

This type is used to imagine what would have been possible if things had turned out differently. In the example, the person speaking entered the Olympics, but did not win a medal.

Always remember that the conditional perfect does not go in the *if* clause. This means it is wrong to say things like *if I'd have had*.

Was/were, should

In formal situations, you should use *were*** instead of *was*** after *if*. This is especially true when you are giving advice. For example: *If I were you, I wouldn't do that.*

You can use *should* instead of *would* when the subject is *I* or *we*. For example: *If I were you, I should stay at home.*

---

in/into

To show that something moves from one place to another, use *into*, especially after the verbs *go, come, walk* and *run*. For example: *Ellie ran into the room.*

To show that something stays in the same place, use *in* (*It is in the corner*).

Lots of verbs can be used with either *in* or *into*, but stick to the rules given above and you will always be right.

Add *in* or *into* to each of these sentences:

1 He could see a girl diving ... the pool.
2 Elaine hurried ... her bedroom.
3 The train had been waiting ... the tunnel for more than half an hour.
4 We went ... the garden to look for worms.
5 I lay ... the bath for forty minutes today.

---

86   *When you talk about facts, rather than conditions, you don't need the conditional tense. For example: *If you heat ice, it melts.*
**These are forms of the verb *to be*.

Split conditionals

Here you can see six sentences which have each been split in two. Put them back together again and match each sentence with the correct picture.

they would not have died.

If I water the plants,

I will bite her.

I would have won.

I will win.

If she had pulled my ear,

I would have bitten her.

If she pulls my ear,

If I had watered the plants,

they will not die.

If I run faster,

If I had run faster,

Dear Maisie

Look at this magazine problem page. Can you replace each number with the correct form of one of the verbs shown here?

to think/to pass/to stop/to be/ to have to/to speak/to eat

HELP!

Dear Maisie,
I failed all my exams again this year, and my teacher says that if I don't work harder, I ..1.. leave the school. But I just can't concentrate.

Switch the TV off and put those magazines away. If you ..2.. your exams the first time, you wouldn't have had these problems.

Dear Maisie,
I want to become a vegetarian, but my mother says if I ..3.. eating meat I will be ill.

Your mother is right to be concerned, but if you ..4.. lots of protein foods you will not be ill.

Dear Maisie,
I have an enormous spot on the end of my nose. I've tried everything, but I just can't get rid of it.

If I ..5.. you, I would try some Wondersqueeze cream. It never fails!

Dear Maisie,
I want to join a tennis club, but I'm very shy. If anyone ..6.. to me, I would turn bright red and start shaking.

In that case, you should definitely join a tennis club. If you do turn red and start shaking, no one ..7.. it is odd: lots of people are very shy.

A wobbly welcome

Barry, the Boppa Breaks holiday rep, has written a welcome note for tourists arriving in Costa Boppa. He has circled a few mistakes that he has made, but is not sure how to correct them. Can you make the necessary corrections?

Hi folks! Welcome to Costa Boppa! This is the world's most remote island: if you (came) by boat it would have taken you thirty-nine hours to get here. But it's also the world's most happening hotspot: if you went to the Costa Brava you (will not find) wilder nightlife.

Costa Boppa is simply gorgeous. If you got up at four o'clock, you (would have seen) some amazing sunrises. If you (wanted) to explore the island a bit, your Boppa Breaks rep will be happy to arrange a bus tour and cultural extravaganza.

If you come on down to the Boppa Breaks karaoke evening tonight, we (would tell) you more about all the great entertainment lined up for you this week.

Well, that's it, folks. If you (will have) any questions, just buzz Larry, Carrie or me, Barry, at the Paradise Club.

To show what someone said, you can either use direct or reported speech. **Direct speech** is when you put the person's exact words in quotation marks ("..."). For example: *Lee said, "I am feeling very tired."*

Reported speech is when you describe what someone said. When you do this, you change the verb into the past tense, even if the information is still true. For example: *Lee said that he was feeling very tired.*

Reporting

To put something like *Ann said, "I cooked this yesterday"* into reported speech, you drop the quotation marks* and make these changes:

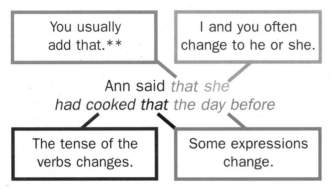

You usually add that.**

I and you often change to he or she.

Ann said *that she had cooked that the day before*

The tense of the verbs changes.

Some expressions change.

Expressions

Here you can see how some common expressions can change when they go into reported speech:

today	that day
yesterday	the day before
tomorrow	the next day
next (week)	the following (week)
last (week)/ a (week) ago	the (week) before
this (week)	that (week)
here	there
this/these	that/those

Tenses

In reported speech, you move the tense of the verbs back into the past and change time expressions.

For example, Vicky says to Alice, "*Ian is taking his exams today*." If Alice wants to report to Debbie what Vicky has said, she should say: "*Vicky said that Ian was taking his exams today*." This applies even if Ian has not actually taken his exams yet.

Here is a summary of how tenses change when verbs go into reported speech:

she ...	I said that she ...
smiles (present simple)	smiled (past simple)
is smiling (present continuous)	was smiling (past continuous)
has smiled, smiled, had smiled (present perfect, past simple, past perfect)	had smiled (past perfect)
will/would smile (future, conditional)	would smile (conditional)

In informal situations it is sometimes acceptable not to change the tense, when you report something that is still true (as in *Melissa said Canada is a great place to live*).

Questions and orders

To report a question (such as *Kate asked, "What are you doing?"*), you take the verb out of its question form, as well as making the usual changes. So you say *Kate asked what I was doing*, not *what was I doing*.

For questions that do not start with words like *what*, *where*, *when* or *why*, you add *if* or *whether*: *He asked if I was ill*.

When you report an order or piece of advice, you normally use the infinitive: *He told me to go home*.

As shown with these examples, with reported questions and orders, you cannot use *said* as the introducing verb. You normally use *asked* in front of a question, and *told*, *advised*, *commanded* or *warned* in front of an order.

On the record

Put these sentences into reported speech, following the guidelines given on this page.

1 Liz said, "I ate Jo's chocolates yesterday."
2 Bobby said to us, "What did you do today?"
3 Carol said, "I am playing squash with my sister today."
4 Neil said, "Has Mandy borrowed my bike?"
5 The teacher said to us, "Never run across the road without looking both ways."

*You also drop the colon (:) or comma (,) that comes in front of what is said.
**After common verbs like *say* and *tell*, you can leave *that* out: *Jo said he had cooked that the week before*.

to/too

To is normally a preposition. You use it to talk about movement from one place to another (as in *I am going to the shops*) and time (*It is five to three*). You use it after certain adjectives (*I am responsible to the manager*) and verbs (*He looks forward to Mondays*). *To* also makes up the infinitive of a verb, as in *to dream*.

Too is an adverb. You use it with other adverbs or adjectives to talk about something that is excessive (more than needed). For example: *He drives too fast*. *Too* is often used with *much* or *many* (*There are too many people*). It can also mean "as well" (*Bob is a teacher, and Shirley is too*).

Write this postcard out, filling the gaps with *to* or *too*.

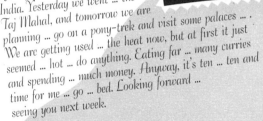

... Ellie,

Having a great time here in India. Yesterday we went ... the Taj Mahal, and tomorrow we are planning ... go on a pony-trek and visit some palaces ... . We are getting used ... the heat now, but at first it just seemed ... hot ... do anything. Eating far ... many curries and spending ... much money. Anyway, it's ten ... ten and time for me ... go ... bed. Looking forward ... seeing you next week.

Much love,
Rob

The Noah C. Parker Interview

Read Noah C. Parker's interview with the soap opera star, I. MacOoldood. Then use it to write down (in full sentences) the star's replies to the questions he was asked.

Noah's natter

Mac told me that he had first decided to be a soap opera star at the age of three. He also told me that he was working on a new soap opera called Suds and Scandal, all about life at a launderette. He said that in his spare time he did a lot of yoga and also knitted his own sweaters. And his real personality? He said he was like all celebrities - the life and soul of parties and lots of fun. Is it true, though, that his best friend is his pet rat? Mac said he had hundreds of friends, but Reginald the rat was great because he never answered back. As for travel, Mac said that he hated foreign food and having to shout to make himself understood. And his ambitions? Mac said that one day he would be the most famous person in the world.

1 When did you decide you wanted to be a soap opera star?
2 What are you working on at the moment?
3 What do you do in your spare time?
4 How would you describe your personality?
5 Is it true that your best friend is your pet rat?
6 Do you like travelling?
7 What are your ambitions?

Drama in Drabsby

Look at this report from the *Drabsby News*, and the reporter's notes on three interviews he has done. Then decide how to fill the gaps in the report. (Follow the rules on reported speech on page 88.)

Drama in Drabsby

The world-famous painting Los Forreva has been snatched from Drabsby Museum by a gang of cunning crooks. Last week's theft was discovered by curator Ivor Topjob. He said that he ..1.. at the museum at quarter past nine, and that he ..2.. at once that Los Forreva ..3.. . Extraordinarily, there appears to be no sign of any break-in. Detective B. Wildered, investigating this mysterious case, said he ..4.. so baffled by a crime, but stressed that he ..5.. into every possibility. Caretaker Luke Safteritt, who said that he ..6.. the museum as usual at half past six ..7.., insists that it was all locked up. He said that he ..8.. a door or window of the museum unlocked in all his time ..9.. . However, Ivor Topjob said that he ..10.. a few questions to ask the caretaker ..11..

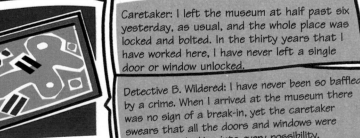

Caretaker: I left the museum at half past six yesterday, as usual, and the whole place was locked and bolted. In the thirty years that I have worked here, I have never left a single door or window unlocked.

Detective B. Wildered: I have never been so baffled by a crime. When I arrived at the museum there was no sign of a break-in, yet the caretaker swears that all the doors and windows were locked. I am looking into every possibility.

Curator: I arrived at the museum at about quarter past nine, opened up, and realized at once that Los Forreva had gone. There were no broken windows or doors, though: I will have a few questions to ask the caretaker today.

Negative niggles

A **negative sentence** contains a negative word such as *not*, *nobody*, *nothing* or *never*. Be careful not to use two negative words, as this makes a sentence positive. For example: *Nobody* did *nothing* means everybody did something. The correct negative sentence is *Nobody did anything*.

When you use *not* with the infinitive of a verb (such as *to run*), it must go in front of *to*. (Otherwise you would be splitting the infinitive, see page 74.) For example: *Try* <u>not</u> *to run*.

Pronoun problems

The pronouns *it* and *you* can be subjects or objects. The others are more tricky: you use *I, he, she, we* and *they* as subjects (as in *I smiled at Jo*), but *me, him, her, us* and *them* as objects (*Jo smiled at* <u>me</u>). These hints will help you know which to use:

1 Use object pronouns after a preposition: *Tom is working <u>with me</u> today.*

2 Use subject pronouns after *as* and *than* if they are followed by a verb. For example: *I am older than <u>he is</u>*. When there is no verb, it is common to use object pronouns: *I am older than <u>him</u>*, although in formal situations people might say: *I am older than <u>he</u>*.

3 When the subject or object is two words joined by *and*, make sure you use the correct pronoun. For example: *Maria and <u>I</u>* (subject) *are visiting Paul*, but *Paul is visiting Maria and <u>me</u>* (object).

Bothers with "be"

People often use the wrong form of *to be*. For example, they say *you <u>was</u>* instead of *you <u>were</u>*. Here are the right forms:

Present simple	Past simple
I am you/we/they are he/she/it is	I was* you/we/they were he/she/it was

Trouble with "them"

Never use *them* instead of *those* in front of a noun. You should say *Pass me <u>those</u> keys*, NOT *Pass me <u>them</u> keys*.

*After *if*, it is sometimes correct to say *I were*. For example: *If I were you, I would not do that*. There is more about this on page 86.

The Supertone chair

Get rid of the mistakes in this advertisement by replacing eight words with the ones listed on the yellow note (use each once only).

Supertone!

**Ever wanted to look really great?
But not had no idea how to lose weight?
Sick of them diets and talk of fresh air?
Well, do it at home: buy a Supertone chair!**

○ You don't need to get out no jogging suit.
○ You don't need to eat no salads or fruit.
○ Just sit in your Supertone chair twice a day, and watch all them surplus pounds slip away.
○ You won't never have looked quite so good, that's for sure.
○ Nothing don't work like the Supertone cure.
○ Enjoy yourself, eat ice cream and curries.
○ With the Supertone chair, no one has no worries.

ever - any - your - any - those - any - those - can

Pronoun puzzler

Write out these sentences, adding one of the pronouns given in brackets.

1 Someone has invited ... and his cousin to go to Japan. (he/him)
2 You know more about it than ... do. (I/me)
3 I hope Gary will dance with ... . (we/us)
4 Paula and ... are going out for lunch. (I/me)
5 Her brother is almost as tall as ... . (she/her)

A letter home

Write out Lucy's letter, correcting the seven mistakes she has made.

Dear Ben,
Thanks very much for the comics you sent me: they was really funny. My Dad and me went ice-skating last week, and he kept falling over. I was desperately trying to not burst out laughing. My exams start next week, but I'm trying to not think about them. Otherwise I haven't really got nothing to tell you. Don't forget to send me them photos you took when we was at the fair last week.
Lots of love,
Lucy

Page 67

Jumbled nouns

The unscrambled nouns are:
1 Paris (**Pisar**)   6 van (**nav**)
2 cleaners (**ranclees**)   7 dogs (**sodg**)
3 painting (**gnapinit**)   8 prison (**rosnip**)
4 policeman (**clamponie**) 9 tourists (**russitot**)
5 doors (**rodos**)

Give and take

A They had bought the **rusty** old car in **Bangkok**.
B Where is **Sarah** today?
C Outside the house stood a shiny **black bicycle**.
D I'm too **busy** to take the **dog** for a walk today.

Pages 68-69

Pronoun fillers

1 it   4 we   7 she
2 he   5 them   8 me
3 I   6 us   9 her

Identity parade

Verbs:	Nouns:	Words that can be either:
follow,	window,	scream,
undo,	desk,	study,
add,	shirt,	hope,
wander,	drawer,	fly,
write	girl	climb

1 My sister is hoping to **study** law at university.
2 We managed to **climb** up onto the ridge of the mountain.
3 Her only **hope** now is that the train is running late.
4 When the man jumped out from behind the door,
   she let out a loud **scream**.
5 Mark swatted the **fly** that kept buzzing around the room.

Sentence spinner

The five sentences you can find are:
I have won a bronze medal.
It was following the young girl.
We are catching an early plane.
They bought a black dog.
She knows the tall man.
It was following the young girl still makes sense when
the object and subject are swapped over: *The young
girl was following it.*

A sack of words

Nouns: postcard, song, Louise, computer, beauty
Verbs: will buy, to cry, is working, to dream, waited
Adjectives: unhappy, sunny, loud
Pronouns: she, we, they, you
Articles: an, the, a

affect/effect

Affect is a verb. *Effect* is usually a noun.
1 What is the **effect** of adding flour to water?
2 That film was really good. There were lots of
   special **effects**.
3 I had a cold, but it didn't really **affect** me very badly.
4 Her illness had a very bad **effect** on her exam
   results.
5 The weather can **affect** the way you feel.

Pages 70-71

Scrambled - after, between, across, into, under

1 My car was parked **between** the truck and
   the motorbike.
2 They walked home **after** the party.
3 The dog jumped **into** the lake.
4 The prisoner ran as fast as he could **across**
   the bridge.
5 The money was hidden **under** the bed.

Sentence building

He couldn't remember her name, **although** he had
met her before.
He forced the door open **and** crept quietly into the
house.
Michelle rushed to the window and looked for the
car, **but** it had already gone.
I can't play tennis today **because** my knee hurts.
She listened to music on her headphones **while**
she was jogging.

Sentence parts

1 (The) / dog / (ran) / (into) / (the) / (road) /
   (and) / (the) / car /(just) / (missed) / (it.)
2 (We)/ (are having) / (a) / (big) /(party,) / (so) /
   (you) / (must come.)
3 (The) / (big) / bear / (escaped) / (from) / (the) /
   (zoo) /(and) / (was) / (never) / seen / (again.)
4 (The) / dancers /(were) /(so) / (shocked) /
   (they) / (had to stop) / (the) / (show.)

borrow/lend; teach/learn

Fill the gap

1 muddy   6 creaky   11 cheerful
2 loud   7 lightly   12 merrily
3 quietly   8 faint   13 thankfully
4 empty   9 deeply
5 heavily   10 suddenly

Pages 72-73

Sentence-splitting

Here you can see where you should have broken up
the sentences (losing *but* and *and*):
... for the past three **weeks**. **She** refused to ...
... with crisps and fizzy **drinks**. **They** don't get ...

Clause spotting

Main clauses: She phoned the police/They arrived/my friend kept a stick insect/One day he let it out
Subordinate clauses: which squashed the poor stick insect/which had incredibly long legs/while Mrs. Kettani was in her garden/because she was terrified of large insects
Phrases: in a fast car/In the house next door/in a panic/in the street

    In the house next door my friend kept a stick insect which had incredibly long legs. One day he let it out in the street while Mrs. Kettani was in her garden. She phoned the police in a panic because she was terrified of large insects. They arrived in a fast car which squashed the poor stick insect.

Sentence stretch

Here are some examples of the most likely extended sentences.

1   The **hungry** monkey **greedily** ate six bananas **when the zookeeper had gone**.
2   She **often** eats at the **Chinese** restaurant **where her brother is a waiter**.
3   He **stupidly** drove the **new** car into a ditch, **because he was fiddling with the radio**.
4   Joanna **slowly** walked up to the **young** horse **which had thrown her off its back**.

an/a

1   He gave me **a** used railway ticket.
2   Jill said she had seen **a** UFO.
3   They gave her **an** X-ray and said she'd be fine.
4   From his window he has **an** incredible view over New York.
5   This is **a** one-way street.
6   Sometimes, a friend can turn into **an** enemy.
7   It was such **a** hot day.
8   It was **an** honest answer.
9   He has **an** older brother.

Pages 74-75

Splitting up

You can finish all the food in the freezer, except for the chocolate cake I made for Dad's birthday, and the leg of lamb, which I'd like you **to take out on Saturday, please**. Also, before Mr. Hopkins drops by on Wednesday, I'd like you **to hoover the sitting room thoroughly**. Could you remember **to water the tomatoes regularly**? By the way, I told Mary you'd try **to drop in on her quickly**.
Before you go out, remember **to double-lock the door carefully**.
Please don't forget to put Bingo out before you go to bed. You need **to feed my goldfish every night**. See you on Saturday - we're going **to try to get the afternoon train if possible**. Perhaps you could pick us up from the station if we give you a ring?

Picture puzzlers

The sentences that match the left-hand pictures are:
1   The girl with the dog gave the envelope to the man.
2   The man who was wearing blue beat his rival.
3   The plant was in the corner of the room with the yellow flowers.
4   Jane rested her foot, which was shaking, on the top rung of the ladder.
The sentences that match the right-hand pictures are:
1   The girl gave the envelope to the man with the dog.
2   The man beat his rival, who was wearing blue.
3   The plant with the yellow flowers was in the corner of the room.
4   Jane rested her foot on the top rung of the ladder, which was shaking.

Adverb adding

1A He's **just** told me I will have to take it easy for a few days.
1B He's told me I will **just** have to take it easy for a few days.
1C He's told me I will have to take it easy **just** for a few days or for **just** a few days.
2A There were **only** a few chocolates left, but Sue ate two.
2B There were a few chocolates left, but Sue **only** ate two.
2C There were a few chocolates left, but **only** Sue ate two.

their/they're/there

1   There **are seven people** in a netball team.
2   Their **dog is** outside.
3   They're **still** in the swimming pool.
4   Their **lawyer is on his** way.
5   Isn't she there **any more**?
6   They're **away** on holiday.

Pages 76-77

Island mission

HERE YOU CAN SEE WHAT IVOR CUNNINGPLAN'S INSTRUCTIONS SAY WHEN THEY ARE PIECED TOGETHER:
YOUR MISSION IS TO DELIVER THE SILICON DOCUMENTS TO THE LEADER OF THE SNEAK STREET GANG.
FIRST GO TO THE ISLANDS OF SKEE-MING, WHICH LIE IN THE WYLIN OCEAN. THEN HEAD FOR THE CITY OF SKA-LEE-WAGS, WHICH IS ON THE NORTHERNMOST ISLAND. ONCE THERE, YOU WILL EASILY LOCATE SNEAK STREET.
ON FRIDAY NIGHT, FIVE MEMBERS OF THE GANG ARE MEETING ON THE CORNER OF SNEAK STREET. EACH MEMBER KNOWS THAT THE DOCUMENTS ARE BEING DELIVERED BY A MAN WITH A LIMP. WALK UP TO THE GANG. IF SOMEONE SAYS: "HERE COME ART FULFOX AND HIS DOG," THEN IT IS NOT SAFE TO DELIVER THE DOCUMENTS. IF SOMEONE SAYS: "HERE COMES ART FULFOX," YOU CAN DROP THEM OFF AND RETURN TO HQ.

Beach breaks

You will take exit C.
The matched-up sentences you will make are:
   The sausages and chicken are on the barbecue.
   A few of the gang were playing volleyball.
   Everyone was enjoying themselves.
   A box of sandwiches was lying in the sand.
   One of our comics was blowing into
   the sea.
   My shorts were covered in chocolate.
   Each of them has bought a different ice cream.
   Catherine and her sister are here.
   Many people are in the sea.

off/of

Sentences 1, 3, 4 and 6 are missing *of*.
Sentences 2, 5 and 7 are missing *off*.

Fill the gaps

1   There **were/are** layers of dust on the piano.
2   "Here **are** Ann and Graham!" she shrieked, pointing across the street.
3   A little bit of money **goes** a long way.
4   When we got back, there **was** a bucketful of tomatoes on the doorstep.
5   Most motorbikes arc cheaper than cars and **go/are** much faster.
6   Success **is/was** more important to him than happiness.

Pages 78-79

like/as

It was so hot, it felt just **like** summer.
The city was just **as** it had always been.
Andy looks **like** my cousin.
Rachael's dog was **like** a large black sheep.
Her head felt **as if** it was about to explode.
After her illness, she looked **like** an old lady.

Tense trippers

Monday
Just before lunch Stuart got a puncture. No one had a puncture repair kit, so we **had** to walk miles to the nearest town. When we finally got there, someone directed us to a bike shop, so we **went** all the way there and then **found** it was closed.

Tuesday
The day went well until we **got** caught behind a herd of sheep on a narrow lane. It took us two hours to get past them, so by the time we got to the youth hostel, it **was** completely full.

Wednesday
Stopped for lunch in a little village. Left our bikes by the church, went to a café, and when we **came** out, Sheila's bike **had** disappeared. Then suddenly we spotted the local vicar riding the missing bike, so we **flagged** him down and he explained everything. The poor vicar sold his own bike a year ago, but he keeps forgetting, so every time he sees a black bike he **thinks** it's his.

Thursday
Arrived at the station to get the train home. We loaded our bikes on board and then **went** for a coffee while we **were** waiting. Suddenly, Stuart noticed that the train was leaving! We **had put** OR We'**d put** our bikes on the wrong one!

Which is which?

have crashed	will understand	invaded
smiled	did not arrive	sing
had promised	buys	had painted
sit	has spotted	
had visited	will drive	

Getting snappy

The photos should be arranged in this order:
Caption A: 1, 2, 3
Caption B: 3, 1, 2
Caption C: 2, 1, 3
Caption D: 2, 3, 1

Pages 80-81

Lost for words

Andrew's desk

He has blown out the candle.
He has broken a glass.
He has eaten an apple.
He has written a letter.
In the afternoon, he blew out the candle.
In the afternoon, he broke a glass.
In the afternoon, he ate an apple.
In the afternoon, he wrote a letter.

Tense trouble

1   They will have to tidy up the house before their parents **get back**.
2   Oliver had just finished writing when the examiner **told** them to put down their pens.
3   Lots of people **will visit** the exhibition when it opens next month.
4   I was furious because the train **was** late.
5   She **went** to Hong Kong last year.
6   They **have lived** in New York for two years, and have no plans to move away.

can/may/might

1   I am very glad that Jenny **can** speak French.
2   You **can** spend as much money as you like OR You **may** spend as much money as you like.
3   **Can** I borrow a pencil? OR **May** I borrow a pencil?
4   **May** I phone my parents? OR **Might** I phone my parents?
5   I might go and see a film this afternoon, if it carries on raining OR I **may** go and see a film this afternoon, if it carries on raining.

Pages 82-83

Identity crisis

1 The fridge is full of bacon. (**which I eat everyday**)
2 The ring which he gave me was far too big.
3 The policeman who drove them home was very friendly.
4 My brother is getting married. (**who is a vet**)
5 The boat had been underwater for thirty years. (**which was found by a diver**)

Who or *whom*?

1 The friend with **whom** I went to Egypt has sent me a letter.
2 The people **who** took the other path got there first.
3 Valerie, **who** has just come back from Mexico, speaks fluent Spanish.
4 This is Jo, **whom** I met on the bus OR **who** I met on the bus.

Murder at Snoot Towers

1	which	4	who	7	which
2	who	5	whom	8	whom/that
3	that/which	6	whose	9	that

Hugo Batty murdered Lord Snoot, whom he was blackmailing. Here you can see how he managed to slip unnoticed from the library to the conservatory, by going through the gardens, the nursery and the breakfast room:

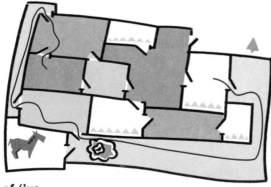

of/'ve

1 "She **must've** decided not to take her car, because I saw it parked in our street this morning."
2 "You really **should've** gone to the party: it was great fun."
3 "We **could've** driven a bit faster, but not much, as the roads are very wet."
4 "If it hadn't been raining, I **would've** come."

Who's who and what's what?

1 The girl **who is swimming** is near the boat.
2 The dog **which is running** has black paws.
3 The ice cream **which the boy is holding** is chocolate and vanilla.
4 The boy **who is running** has red hair.
5 The cow **the policeman is chasing** has black ears.
6 The dog **which is swimming** is near the boat.
7 The baby **the woman is holding** has a pink hat.
8 The man **whom the policeman is chasing** has a red sweater.

Pages 84-85

Comparing climates

1 In August, Weatherchester is **hotter** than Seasonbury.
2 In January, Weatherchester is **colder** than Seasonbury.
3 In March, Seasonbury is **drier** than Weatherchester.
4 In September, Seasonbury is **wetter** than Weatherchester.

Character questionnaire

Jon is more patient than Tessa.
Jon is lazier than Tessa.
Tessa is friendlier than Jon.
Jon is more careful than Tessa.
Tessa is nosier than Jon.
Jon is more selfish than Tessa.

Quite/quiet

1 You look **quite** washed out.
2 As Stefan walked **past**, he noticed the man's gun.
3 It is very **quiet** without Diane and Vicky.
4 Veronica was so happy when she **passed** her exams.
5 In the **past** week, I have lost two umbrellas.
6 I have always found maths **quite** hard.

Moped mania

The Superwhizz is wider than the Pipsqueak.
The Superwhizz is longer than the Pipsqueak.
The Superwhizz is more expensive than the Pipsqueak.
The Superwhizz is faster than the Pipsqueak.
The Superwhizz is heavier than the Pipsqueak.
The Stumbly is wider than the Featherzoom.
The Featherzoom is longer than the Stumbly.
The Featherzoom is more expensive than the Stumbly.
The Featherzoom is faster than the Stumbly.
The Stumbly is heavier than the Featherzoom.
The Thriftyshift is wider than the Pipsqueak.
The Thriftyshift is longer than the Pipsqueak.
The Pipsqueak is more expensive than the Thriftyshift.
The Pipsqueak is faster than the Thriftyshift.
The Pipsqueak is heavier than the Thriftyshift.
The fastest moped Sally can buy is a Pipsqueak.

Of the two faster mopeds, the Superwhizz is too expensive, and the Featherzoom is too long.

Pages 86-87

in/into

1 He could see a girl diving **into** the pool.
2 Elaine hurried **into** her bedroom.
3 The train had been waiting **in** the tunnel for more than half an hour.
4 We went **into** the garden to look for worms.
5 I lay **in** the bath for forty minutes today.

Split conditionals

1 If I had watered the plants, they would not have died.
2 If I water the plants, they will not die.
3 If she pulls my ear, I will bite her.
4 If she had pulled my ear, I would have bitten her.
5 If I had run faster, I would have won.
6 If I run faster, I will win.

Dear Maisie

1 will have to
2 had passed
3 stop
4 eat
5 were
6 spoke
7 will think

A wobbly welcome

Hi folks! Welcome to Costa Boppa! This is the world's most remote island: if you **had come** by boat it would have taken you thirty-nine hours to get here. But it's also the world's most happening hotspot: if you went to the Costa Brava you **would not find** wilder nightlife.

Costa Boppa is simply gorgeous. If you got up at four o'clock, you **would see** some amazing sunrises. If you **want** to explore the island a bit, your Boppa Breaks rep will be happy to arrange a bus tour and cultural extravaganza.

If you come on down to the Boppa Breaks karaoke evening tonight, we **will tell** you more about all the great entertainment lined up for you this week. Well, that's it, folks. If you **have** any questions, just buzz Larry, Carrie or me, Barry, at the Paradise Club.

Pages 88-89

On the record

1 Liz said (that) she had eaten Jo's chocolates the day before yesterday.
2 Bobby asked us what we had done that day.
3 Carol said (that) she was playing squash with her sister that day.
4 Neil asked whether Mandy had borrowed his bike OR Neil asked if Mandy had borrowed his bike.
5 The teacher warned us never to run across the road without looking both ways.

to/too

To Ellie,
Having a great time here in India. Yesterday we went **to** the Taj Mahal, and tomorrow we are planning **to** go on a pony-trek and visit some palaces **too**. We are getting used **to** the heat now, but at first it just seemed **too** hot **to** do anything. Eating far **too** many curries and spending **too** much money. Anyway, it's ten **to** ten and time for me **to** go **to** bed. Looking forward **to** seeing you next week.
Much love,
Rob

The Noah C. Parker interview

1 I first decided to be a soap opera star at the age of three.
2 I am working on a new soap opera called Suds and Scandal, all about life at a launderette.
3 In my spare time I do a lot of yoga and also knit my own sweaters.
4 I am like all celebrities - the life and soul of parties and lots of fun.
5 I have hundreds of friends, but Reginald the rat is great because he never answers back.
6 I hate foreign food and having to shout to make myself understood.
7 One day I will be the most famous person in the world.

Drama in Drabsby

1 had arrived
2 had realized
3 had gone
4 had never been
5 was looking
6 had left
7 the day before
8 had never left
9 there
10 would have
11 that day

Page 90

The Supertone chair

Ever wanted to look really great?
But not had **any** idea how to lose weight?
Sick of **those** diets and talk of fresh air?
Well, do it at home: buy a Supertone chair!
You don't need to get out **your** jogging suit.
You don't need to eat **any** salads or fruit.
Just sit in your Supertone chair twice a day,
and watch all **those** surplus pounds slip away.
You won't **ever** have looked quite so good, that's for sure.
Nothing **can** work like the Supertone cure.
Enjoy yourself, eat ice cream and curries.
With the Supertone chair, no one has **any** worries.

Pronoun puzzler

1 Someone has invited **him** and his cousin to go to Japan.
2 You know more about it than **I** do.
3 I hope Gary will dance with **us**.
4 Paula and **I** are going out for lunch.
5 Her brother is almost as tall as **her** (OR **she** - very formal).

A letter home

Dear Ben,
Thanks very much for the comics you sent me: they **were** really funny. My Dad and **I** went ice-skating last week, and he kept falling over. I was desperately trying **not to** burst out laughing. My exams start next week, but I'm trying **not to** think about them. Otherwise I haven't really got **anything** OR **much** to tell you. Don't forget to send me **those** photos you took when we **were** at the fair last week.
Lots of love,
Lucy

This edition was first published in 1997 by Usborne Publishing Ltd, Usborne House, 83-85 Saffron Hill, London, EC1N 8RT, England. www.usborne.com Copyright © 2003, 1997, 1995, 1994. Usborne Publishing Ltd.

Books are to be returned on or before

birth to three

supporting our youngest children

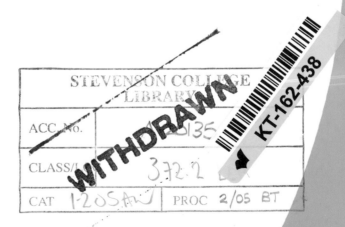

Acknowledgements

Grateful thanks go to all those who have contributed their thoughts and suggestions, to the individuals and organisations who have provided ideas for examples from practice, and to all those who have helped to gather the many photographs used in this document.

First published 2005

© Learning and Teaching Scotland 2005

ISBN 1 84399 061 X

Contents

Throughout this document, the terms 'staff' and 'adult' have been used to include all adults working with babies and young children.

Throughout this document, the term 'every child' includes children with diverse cultural backgrounds, children with physical and sensory impairment and those with recognised health and social needs.

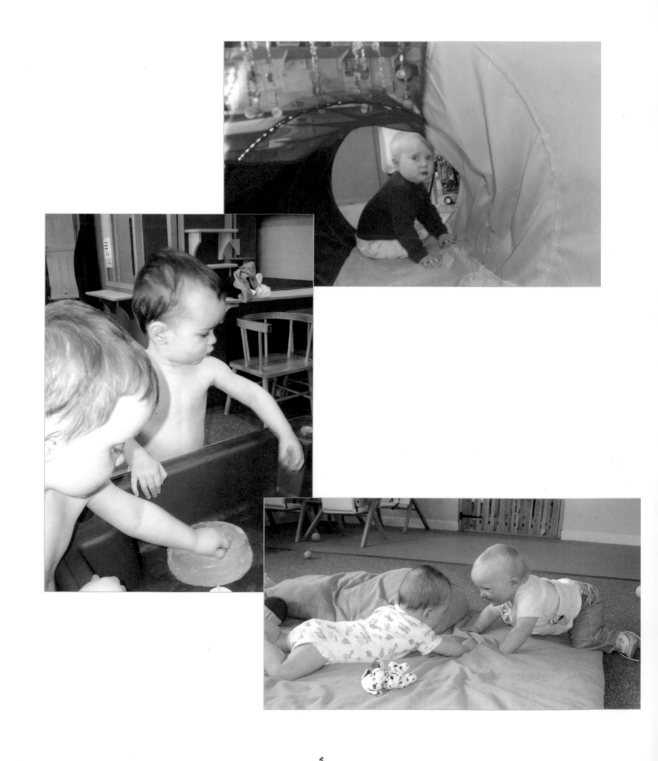

Foreword

Our vision is for a Scotland where every child matters, and where all children experience support enabling them to reach their full potential and giving them the best possible start in life. There is increasing recognition that a child's earliest years are vital in this respect. It is most important that babies and very young children are loved and secure, healthy, and cared for. They also need opportunities to play, develop and learn in a safe environment. This, in turn, will help them develop the self-esteem, confidence, and independence needed to face future challenges.

Birth to Three: supporting our youngest children acts as valuable guidance for all those involved in caring for babies and very young children. This may include early years workers, social care and health practitioners, and students preparing to work in early years settings. It identifies the key features of relationships, responsiveness and respect that support sensitive and well-informed approaches to this age group and beyond.

Birth to Three: supporting our youngest children acts as a foundation for a child's future learning and development, taken forward in *A Curriculum Framework for 3 to 5*, and is based on the same concept that care and learning are inseparable. *Birth to Three: supporting our youngest children* also reflects the view in *For Scotland's Children* that the care and wellbeing of children is the concern of everybody. I commend this important document to all those working with our youngest children, for its guidance and practice examples, and as a tool to stimulate dialogue and reflection between colleagues.

Peter Peacock
Minister for Education and Young People

Section 1
Introduction
Key features of effective practice

We know that children's experiences in their early years are very closely related to the quality of the care that they receive. We also know that these experiences can have a real impact on how children develop in the future.

It is important that all those involved in the wellbeing, care and education of babies and young children have guidance that sets a context for high-quality care and education and which identifies key features that support and promote sensitive and well-informed approaches.

This guidance is based on three key features through which effective support and learning opportunities for very young children can be developed:

- Relationships
- Responsive care
- Respect.

In practice, these three key features are interrelated, so that although each has a separate section in this guidance, each is linked to the other. Each of these three key features of effective practice reinforces the other and each also has an important influence in its own right. How these features are interpreted in practice is a question for individuals and for teams, for children and for families.

This guidance recognises the different and complementary ways in which very young children are cared for in different settings. It is based on the fundamental understanding that environment, health, community and family all influence children's personal development and shape children's early experiences.

Equally, whilst children's early experiences play a role in shaping their future attitudes and dispositions, we know that children are able individuals in their own right, with the resilience and inner strength to face and overcome many of life's challenges.

Many countries are looking at the area of birth to three because of a growing recognition of the importance of early childhood and family life. Safeguarding children's best interests and insisting on the best are fundamental to meeting the needs of children, their families and everyone involved in young children's wellbeing, care and education. Drawing upon national and international birth to three research and acknowledging notable practices from other countries in caring for young children, this guidance sets out the three key features of effective practice and suggests sensitive and respectful approaches through examples from practice. It is then the responsibility of individuals within their own contexts to interpret and adapt the guidance as a framework for their own practice. It does not provide a list of the right ways to behave and interact with babies and young children, but it does suggest particular approaches and ways of interacting that we know are beneficial, most importantly for the children themselves, but also for the adults responsible for them.

This document can help to:

- get people together, to share ideas and promote partnership
- promote discussion within a staff group
- build confidence, if you are new to working with young children
- allow you time to 'think' and not just 'do' – time to reflect on your role
- act as a tool for raising awareness and promoting collaboration across different sectors
- inform the ways in which you support children and their families
- support you in your role as someone who works with young children.

Shared principles

This document shares the same underlying principles as *A Curriculum Framework for Children 3 to 5.*

The best interests of children

Taking young children's and babies' best interests into account means working closely with parents and with others involved with the child. Close partnerships allow all the important information about a child to be shared, reflected upon and acted upon. The expertise and experience of both parents and early years educators are valuable and they have most value when they are shared. They are equally important.

The central importance of relationships

Relationships are influential. They are the basis not only for effective learning, but also for healthy development and emotional wellbeing. Whether in the home, in the early years setting or in the wider community, relationships are of central importance.

The need for all children to feel included

Children need to have a sense of belonging, a feeling of being welcome and of being important and valued if they are to participate and contribute, feel happy and thrive. Feeling included is supported by the responsive care illustrated in this document. Feeling included is based on mutual respect and on warm, reciprocal relationships.

It is the responsibility of all adults to ensure that children thrive. It is the responsibility of everybody that children grow up both as healthy and as happy as possible.

An understanding of the ways in which children learn

As with older children, the learning process for babies and very young children is complex.

Early learning involves opportunities to play, to interact, to explore, to create and to problem solve.

It is supported by:

- environments that are flexible and responsive, which can adapt to children's immediate interests and needs
- relationships that encourage children to participate actively
- opportunities for children to communicate their feelings and their thoughts, for example through quiet one-to-one times with an important adult
- adults who are interested and attentive.

Although we do not fully understand yet the ways in which learning takes place, we know it is complex. Young children learn in many different ways. To respond to children's learning adults need to be closely observant, to be flexible in the ways in which they respond, and to trust children as capable and competent learners.

Equality, inclusion and diversity

This guidance is also based on the fundamental principle of equality of opportunity. An inclusive approach is essential to the provision of high-quality care and education for all young children and their families. Inclusive practices benefit all children.

Inclusion is about working closely with parents and carers, being able to take different approaches to fit individual circumstances and valuing that everyone involved with children and families has an important contribution to make, particularly the child and the family themselves. It recognises that diversity is something to be valued, that children and families have many different and changing needs and that irrespective of needs, the key features of relationships, responsive care and respect apply to every child.

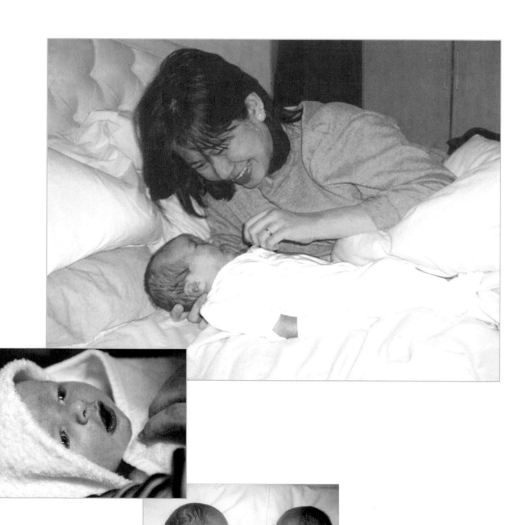

Section 2
The importance of early experiences

Human beings are active participants in the world around them from the moment they are born.

We know that for babies and young children, care and learning are not two separate things. Some of the approaches that clearly recognise the ways in which young children learn throughout their day, are illustrated in later sections contained in this document.

It is important to have an understanding of patterns of development, but it is even more important to be aware that each child progresses at his or her own pace and develops at a different rate and in different ways from any other child. This guidance is based on the understanding that children are unique individuals – active participants in all that happens around them – with particular needs, interests, preferences and capabilities. This requires flexibility, a willingness to adapt and the ability to act upon what you know and what you find out, rather than what you might expect because of a child's age.

All children have their own pattern of development. Although research has identified what are often referred to as 'norms of development', babies and young children need to be allowed the time and the support necessary for their own personal development.

Babies and young children as learners

Because of research, we know that babies are born with what is referred to as a 'predisposition' – a natural inclination for learning. They are eager to learn and to make sense of their world. All babies are different and employ a range of senses and abilities to investigate the world they live in, to communicate with others, to adjust to different people and surroundings and to form relationships. Within the first three years of life, most babies quickly learn to interact with others around them, to walk, to talk and to solve problems at a truly amazing rate.

Research into brain development in recent years has established that:

- learning takes place within the womb before a baby is even born
- babies are born with a powerful motivation and ability to learn
- young children's brains develop very rapidly and the responses that babies and young children receive from the others around them actively promote this rapid development
- from birth, babies' brains are ready to begin making connections and many important connections are made in the first three years of life
- by being active and involved, by learning through exploration, discovery and interactions with others, development takes place.

Birth to three is not just a step along the way towards becoming a person, but an exciting time in a child's development, which deserves to be recognised and celebrated in its own right.

Young children need intimate and flexible environments, with *other people*, who will give them time and attention, who will show a genuine interest and delight in them, who are able to shown an enthusiasm and a willingness to be adaptable and who demonstrate that children's feelings and ideas matter.

Research has important implications for the ways in which adults support, care and provide for very young children. It reminds us that it is important not to underestimate the competence of even the youngest child. It encourages us to trust children and to allow them opportunities to show just how capable and knowledgeable they are, rather than assuming that, because they are very small, they are not able to do things. Babies and young children learn positively and begin to make sense of the world through warm and accepting relationships, through enjoyable play and from being involved in everyday routines. Although young children have similar basic needs, all babies and children are unique individuals. Understanding what is unique about each child you care for allows you to meet children's needs in the special and individual way that supports the individual's development and learning.

For example, all babies and children need food, warmth, affection and stimulation. However, there will be many variations in the way that individual babies like to be fed and differences in what they like to eat; there will be differences in the way that babies allow themselves to be comforted and soothed and differences in the ways that babies ask for and accept affection. There will be differences in the ways and the pace at which they learn. This is because they are all individuals and one approach for all will not be appropriate or effective.

Environments

Environments matter. Early care has long-lasting effects and young children are very sensitive to the atmosphere and environment around them. It is important that the environments that children find themselves in have the right ingredients to allow them to grow and to thrive.

The environment includes everything to do with the child's surroundings, both indoors and outdoors. It includes what children are exposed to in terms of lifestyle patterns, such as a healthy diet and opportunities for exercise and fresh air. Even before a baby is born, the environment that the pregnant mother is in plays an important role. Access to a healthy lifestyle, including diet, exercise, hazard-free surroundings and the right kind and amount of support and attention, is known to make a difference to maternal health and to the unborn child.

The environment includes the adults around the child. Children learn in a variety of ways, including through playful exploration and through their interactions with others. Adults who are active and involved, who understand when to interact with children and when to step back, are an essential part of the environment.

Babies and young children learn from the environment they are in from:

* the attitudes and values of the adults in the environment, for example the way in which they are greeted at the beginning of the day and the way in which staff members talk to one another

- other children in the environment, both older and younger
- the play opportunities and resources available to them
- the space available to them and how this is used
- routines, for example nappy changing, hand washing, lunch time and the experience of being dropped off and collected at the end of the day
- daily opportunities for interaction, discovery, active learning, talk and exploration, in spacious, carefully arranged areas both indoors and outside.

Young children develop and learn most happily in an environment that is full of opportunities for them to explore, create and follow their own particular interests. The role of an interested, affectionate, reliable and consistent adult is central to supporting young children's investigations, together with genuine, two-way conversations.

Babies and young children need environments where they:

- feel safe, but not overprotected to the point where experiences are unnecessarily restricted, both indoors and outdoors
- feel trustful that their needs will be noticed and responded to
- feel confident that their interests will be supported and valued
- feel a sense of involvement and belonging

where they can:

- be involved in enjoyable, purposeful and creative activity
- be listened to and communicate
- see familiar aspects of the home environment around them that they recognise, such as comfy settees, mirrors, favourite mobiles, and pictures of themselves, their families and their homes
- move between settings, such as home and nursery, with the reassurance that there will be continuity in their experiences and that individual differences will be valued and reflected in what is provided, through the resources available, through display of photographs and through carefully planned activities

and where they:

- begin to learn how to make healthy choices that support their growth and development, such as what to have for a snack, or when to put a coat on
- can develop warm and reciprocal relationships with important adults and with other children, based upon respect and acceptance
- can join in and contribute.

Babies and young children need the sort of environment that is most likely to foster effective and confident child development and to experience an environment of mutual respect and trust and open communication. Where large numbers of children are being cared for together, it is even more important to be aware of the importance of the environment and its influence on children's wellbeing and sense of self.

The environment that children find themselves in helps to create children's sense of personal identity and sense of self-esteem. The environment also helps to establish the right sort of atmosphere for children to be able to develop and learn.

Developing a sense of self

The people around them can help children to feel good about themselves and who they are. This is important because children's early experiences of being loved and being lovable have a direct influence on their self-esteem and sense of wellbeing as they develop and grow.

This means that the people around children need to demonstrate:

- warmth
- respect
- understanding
- acceptance of the child, which often means needing to separate feelings about a child's behaviour from feelings about the child as a person.

Feeling safe, confident and good about themselves is necessary in its own right. It is also necessary if children are to learn effectively.
A Curriculum Framework 3 to 5 for Children, Scottish CCC, 1999

Babies begin to build up a picture of themselves right from the start. These pictures that babies and young children build up of themselves are influenced by the responses and reactions of others.

A Curriculum Framework for Children 3 to 5 rightly places an emphasis upon emotional, personal and social development, areas that remain important not only at the 3–5 stage of children's development, but also at earlier and at later stages of development.

Equally, if adults are to cope with the complex demands of caring for babies and young children, it helps if they feel good in themselves. They too need to feel secure and well supported; they need to be cared for and feel that they are respected in their role.

Supporting young children

The number of books sold in the United Kingdom in 2001 on parenting and how to care for very young children was greater than the number of babies actually born in that year.[1] This seems to indicate at the very least an interest in the subject, and perhaps even a degree of anxiety. Regardless, it begins to illustrate the fact that people feel they need to be informed about how to be an adult who cares for very young children.

What may seem like common sense to one person may not appear so to another and it is important that intuition – the feeling that something is 'right' – is informed intuition. Informed intuition is based upon both knowledge and experience. It is gained through opportunities for hands-on participation and observation, through training and development opportunities and through

[1] *The Independent on Sunday* 16 February 2003

opportunities to reflect and discuss. Informed intuition allows you to understand why you do things in certain ways and it allows you to explain and to share why you do things in certain ways with others.

This is important, whether you are a practitioner involved with children and their families, an early years educator working in a nursery, playgroup, or your own home, or a student just beginning to learn about the needs of very young children. It is important to get the balance right between what is often referred to as common sense and recognising that common sense alone is not all that is required in order to meet the wide-ranging and complex needs of babies and young children.

There are many skills involved in working with and caring for young children, which all adults need. These include:

- experience and the support to reflect and learn from experience
- confidence and the ability to respond in the best possible ways to individual children
- really knowing about the child, trusting that knowledge and the judgments that are based on this
- being prepared to learn from the child, for example by listening to what a child tells you and observing what they do.

Supporting babies and young children – as they begin to learn about the world around them, the people who are significant to them, and themselves above all – is most effective when adults are aware of the crucial role of the three key features of effective practice – relationships, responsive care and respect.

Section 3

Relationships – promoting effective practice

Relationships are influential. They provide the basis for young children's development and learning.

Building effective relationships is one key feature in ensuring effective practice with young children and their families, together with the key features of responsive care and respect.

Key considerations for establishing effective relationships include:

- providing opportunities to establish warm and affectionate bonds with significant people
- providing opportunities to interact with others, both adults and children
- maintaining respectful and inclusive partnerships between all those involved with the child
- developing environments that promote security and consistency
- developing environments that promote trust and understanding.

Key to making the most of children's capabilities is the quality of the warm, affectionate and responsive relationships surrounding babies and young children. Children become confident, independent and most resilient where they are secure in the relationships around them.

The central importance of relationships

Relationships begin before a baby is born. They begin with the care and attention that babies receive while they are in the womb. Because of this, babies are born already strongly connected to other people. The important process of attachment and forming relationships has begun even before they are born.

'Bonding' is the term that is commonly used to describe the deep and powerful attachment between a baby and the important people in the baby's life.

It used to be thought that babies really only bonded with their mothers but we now know that babies can bond to a number of important or significant people. Babies can form an attachment with a variety of others, including:

- their mother and father
- their grandparents
- their brothers and sisters
- their foster carer
- those who care for them outside the home.

Although newborn babies are eager to interact with others, the process of bonding is a gradual one. Relationships take time to become established, because they are based on a growing understanding of one another.

The central importance of relationships is recognised in many of today's care and education practices, through environments:

- where space is carefully arranged to encourage the development of relationships, the opportunity to explore and the chance to be in inviting, cosy areas
- that reflect the importance of the child's home and community

through practices that:

- encourage parental involvement, such as informal drop-ins, open evenings and events, displays and newsletters
- encourage interagency working, where staff from different sectors work together to support young children and their families, through joint meetings and exchanges of information

and through policies that:

- include well-thought-out key-person systems that provide continuity, someone for children and their parents to get to know well, and a back-up person in case that special person cannot be there
- support settling in and transitions, such as inviting parents to stay with their child, asking parents advice on whether the child has a favourite object such as a teddy or a blanket that will help the child to settle into new surroundings or provide comfort if distressed.

Developing relationships

Newborn babies are skilled, not only at responding to others but also at initiating interactions themselves. The ability to establish and maintain relationships is, of course, a lifelong process, but one that we can see beginning even in the first few days and weeks of life.

- Newborn babies have a fascination with the human face and will spend long stretches of time simply gazing at the face of the adult holding them.
- Even babies a few minutes old focus intently on the face of another person and can attempt to imitate facial expressions and sounds.
- As early as 3 months, babies can be seen to respond to gestures and to use body language and sounds purposefully in order to attract attention, and communicate.
- Even earlier than 3 months, babies are demonstrating their interest in communicating and in the conversations of those around them.

Young babies are also very interested in other babies and children.

Relationships are built as individuals get to know, trust and understand one another. Relationships are built by taking the time to listen, by welcoming smiles and comments, and through showing understanding and acceptance of individual circumstances

Opportunities for children to interact with one another and with older and younger children are important. Children's relationships and friendships have an important role in supporting children through transitions and in coping with new situations, such as the birth of a sibling.

Babies and young children are very perceptive and aware of the feelings and atmosphere around them. Relationships between adults and children, between adults and other adults and between children themselves all have an important role to play in developing the young child's sense of self and their understanding of how to interact with others.

Good relationships help to encourage, maintain and promote other good relationships.

Consistently warm and secure relationships are of central importance if children are to be able to:

- communicate their needs and feelings
- rely on others and build up a sense of security and trust
- develop a positive sense of themselves and who they are
- learn to interact in positive ways with others
- develop the skills necessary to cope with conflict, challenges and new situations.

Even in situations where children have been neglected and abused and where the relationships they have experienced are inconsistent and lacking in warmth, research has shown that successfully being able to build a warm, secure and reliable relationship elsewhere can help children to recover.

The resilience or inner strength that children possess has been the subject of much discussion and there are many examples that show us how competent and capable young children can be, even in conditions that are adverse to healthy development and growth. Resilience can be acquired in a number of ways, but key factors could include:

- having the experience of coping with challenging situations
- forming a positive relationship with an adult, not necessarily a parent, who is reliable and unconditionally supportive
- having access to high-quality early years provision that takes account of the needs of the whole child.

Although we cannot always be sure exactly where resilience comes from, there is no doubt that children can be helped to be resilient and resilience can help children to cope with and move on from short-lived adversities experienced in childhood.[2]

[2] Newman, T, Blackburn, S, *Transitions in the Lives of Children and Young People: Resilience Factors*, 2002

Relationships and learning

Children's emotional and social development cannot be separated from their cognitive growth and development. In order to be able to learn effectively, young children need to have the self-belief and knowledge that they can learn; they need to be able to see themselves as competent and capable individuals.

Confidence and self-esteem are both important for learning. Positive, warm and responsive relationships are the key to children's sense of personal identity and self-worth and they are also the key to helping babies and young children to develop and learn. Young children learn, not only from what they see and experience around them, but also from how they are treated.

Through positive personal relationships with others children begin to learn that they are valued and appreciated.

They learn how to:

*   explore their environment confidently
*   communicate and interact
*   be accepted by and accepting of others, which further develops self-confidence and positive relationships
*   make sense of and trust in the reliability of what is expected of them, for example, through consistent and fair expectations and boundaries.

High-quality care and education that supports children's learning involves:

*   recognising that relationships support learning and that they take time to develop
*   acknowledging the close relationships that children already have and valuing the information that comes with the child, about children's likes and dislikes, about the people and things that are important to them
*   being responsive to individual children's needs, interests, preferences and capabilities and ensuring opportunities for the one-to-one time that all children need, by finding time for a cuddle, the time to read a story or the opportunity to sit peacefully and listen to the child talk about something that is of interest to the child
*   focusing on what children can do, taking delight in their achievements and sharing this information with others, including the individual child.

Adults who work with young children need to understand:

*   the significance of a baby's or young child's behaviour, for example that sitting quietly in a corner may be a way of relaxing for one child, but could indicate unhappiness in another
*   their own role in supporting, in a consistent way, young children's understanding of the expectations of their behaviour
*   the importance of using partnerships between home, the community and early years settings to support relationships and to support transitions
*   the diversity of family lifestyles and the significant events in the lives of families.

For babies and young children, learning to form relationships successfully is partly to do with experiencing how people relate to one another.

Sensitive approaches towards relationships

Children's earliest experiences usually take place within the family. Families are complex, and each family is different. Just as each child is a unique individual, each family is also unique. Each family, however it is made up, is extremely important to the child within it. To be effective, adults who work with children and their families need to take into account that it is crucial to be able to engage with parents in all circumstances.

Effective partnership with parents involves fully appreciating that parents have a deep understanding of their own child, from which others need to learn. It involves:

* respecting and valuing the knowledge, skills and experience that parents have
* being non-judgmental and appreciating children's strong feelings about their families
* trying to understand things from a parent's perspective as well as from your own
* valuing the parent's contribution, whatever form that contribution may take.

Parents experience joy and fulfilment as well as disappointment and frustration. Parenting is not an easy or straightforward task. It is full of responsibility and it is sometimes overwhelming. Parents do not become effective parents the moment that a baby arrives. Effective parenting develops and evolves.

Where the care of a child is shared, it is important to get the balance right. It can be hard for parents suddenly to see their child begin to form an important relationship with someone other than themselves. Knowing that children have the ability to attach to more than one significant person in their lives is important, and understanding how important it is that children do become attached to all those involved in their care helps to ensure what is best for the child. Children need to form warm and reciprocal relationships with those involved in their daily lives.

Developing strong and secure relationships with parents is essential for all those involved. Genuine relationships between staff and parents are based on partnership.

This includes:

* finding the time to engage in a genuine dialogue with parents and other carers in order to reassure them and in order to build trust, for example by finding out about their child's personality and what interests them at home
* recognising that parents feel most at ease when they feel that their child is known by all the adults who play a role within the early years setting
* making sure that parents feel confident that their child will be welcomed and valued as an individual.

Building positive personal relationships outside the home requires patience, sensitivity and recognition of all the significant people in a child's life.

For many parents, ensuring that they feel genuinely included relies upon communicating all of the small details of the day, however trivial they might seem. Others, however, may find it difficult to hear all the details of exciting developments made by their child when they were not present. Knowing parents well helps you to tune into their needs and preferences. Taking the right approach with individuals helps parents to feel included, confident and in control.

Sensitive approaches towards parents help to overcome any difficulties associated with shared care and they help to establish mutually respectful relationships.

Sensitive approaches towards parents include:

- understanding the demands on parents, for example, by accepting that all parents cannot and may not wish to be involved in the setting in the same way or to the same degree
- understanding individual circumstances and being respectful of differences
- understanding and responding to the changing needs of parents, for example when there might be change or an upheaval in a family
- understanding that parents may need reassurance with regard to the continuing importance of the parental role.

Sensitive approaches involve:

- communicating sensitively and supportively with parents, even in difficult circumstances, perhaps where their child is being aggressive to others, struggling with tantrums and the desire to get their own way, or not settling well
- sharing important information consistently, through informal chats and more formal meetings
- showing warmth and interest through what you say and what you remember
- creating environments that welcome and value the parental role, for example by having a dedicated space for parents to sit or a parents' room
- ensuring that parents and carers feel comfortable and well informed about transitions that affect their child.

Recognising and respecting that time spent with parents is valuable time is important. Parents know a great deal about their own child and have specific knowledge of their child that others can never have. Early years practitioners and others who work with young children often have in-depth experience of working with many different children. Put together, this knowledge works very effectively in ensuring that the child is understood.

Parents not only benefit from but are entitled to feel included and one way of ensuring this is to consistently share important information with parents, where possible, on a daily basis. There are many ways of doing this, including:

- informal exchanges of information as parents or carers drop off and collect children

- more formal exchanges of information, such as baby care sheets, parent-held records, documented observations of the child during the day and children's profiles
- displays of children's work
- digital photographs of the day's events on display where parents can choose whether to look at them
- video footage, where parents agree, for parents to take home with them of their child that day
- opportunities for parents to spend time in the setting and opportunities for support and discussion with parents within the home.

Sensitive approaches towards children help to build mutually respectful relationships. They reassure children of their own importance.

Sensitive approaches towards children include:

- a genuine acceptance, shown through what adults say and do, but also, importantly, how they say and do it
- valuing the time spent in interactions with the child, rather than being too focused on completing tasks
- providing as integrated a social experience as possible, a sense of togetherness rather than 'them and us'
- making sure that you are available to the child and planning quiet intimate time together
- not spending time with one child to the exclusion of others.

Sensitive approaches involve:

- understanding that children need to feel they are being 'kept in mind'[3] – so that even in the busiest times of the day, young children feel secure that they have not been forgotten: by being given a smile, by being talked to, by being noticed
- understanding the use of physical care can help to build relationships, where it is personalised and attentive to individual needs and preferences
- understanding that children all have their individual pace, which fluctuates and changes, often in the course of just one day
- understanding that there are times when babies and young children wish to be quiet and reflective and to opt out of a busy environment.

All of these approaches to both parents and children need to be underpinned by an awareness of the importance of striking the right balance and building close relationships with children, set within the context of other significant relationships that the child might already have, for example with their parents, their siblings, their grandparents or a carer.

[3] Gillispie Edwards, A, *Relationships and Learning: caring for children from birth to three*, NCB Enterprises Ltd, 2002

Examples from practice

Sensitive approaches towards relationships

Calum, 16 weeks old, is a new arrival at nursery. He is settling well and his key person, Heather, is able to tell Calum's parents that he is content throughout the day.

Calum's mother, however, is distressed each morning as she leaves Calum and tells Heather that she is concerned that Calum is upset during the day and that the nursery is not telling her. Calum's mother has taken to phoning the nursery several times each day from work, asking to speak to Heather. This is not always possible, as Heather is busy and occupied with the children. This is making Calum's mother increasingly concerned.

The nursery manager explains to Calum's mother that Heather is busy with the children and offers to check on Calum herself each day and report back, but Calum's mother prefers to hear directly about Calum's day from Heather.

Heather and the other three members of staff in the baby room, all of whom are building relationships with both Calum and his parents, discuss the situation with the nursery manager and share their views on how well Calum is settling and how best to reassure Calum's mother.

Staff members agree that whilst Calum has settled very well, his mother needs to be reassured of this and needs to feel more included in his day. They decide, with the permission of Calum's parents, to take the opportunity to use the video camera to take footage of Calum at different points each day to give to his mother to take home with her, in addition to the digital photographs on display, so that she is able to see that he is contented and settling well.

Some points to consider

- *Do you think the approach taken helped the relationship between staff and Calum's parents?*
- *What are the likely benefits of involving all staff?*

Working in partnership

Charlene is two and a half and lives with her paternal grandparents due to her mother's ongoing drug problem. The relationship between Charlene's mother and grandparents is very tense and because of this, contact between Charlene and her mother cannot take place in the grandparents' home.

Contact between Charlene and her mother is important however, and therefore has to be made possible elsewhere, somewhere that feels both familiar and comfortable to Charlene.

Charlene has attended a family centre since she was a year old and staff members at the family centre agree to facilitate the contact between Charlene and her mother, by allowing the social worker to bring Charlene's mother into their 'under threes' room. Charlene's mother is unable to go on her own to these visits as she has been intoxicated in the past, which has caused distress for Charlene. With the support of the family centre staff, the social worker can observe the appropriateness of the contact between Charlene and her mother and assess each contact to ensure that each occasion has purpose, meaning and value to Charlene.

The social worker being present also allows him to assess from a distance, as he can be involved in playing with other children in the 'under threes' room, at the same time as observing mother and child in a familiar and usual environment.

Some points to consider

- *Why is it important for Charlene that the contact is taking place in the family centre?*
- *How might the ongoing partnership between the family centre staff and the social worker continue to support Charlene?*

Valuing communication

Craig's mother is concerned that he is very lively when he returns from his childminder in the evening. He will not go to bed when his mother wants him to, so she asks Zara, his childminder, not to let him sleep any more during the day as he does not usually have a sleep at home.

Zara explains that Craig is finding it tiring being with the other children all day and describes the kind of day Craig usually has with her. This often involves several outings, collecting older children from school, going to playgroup and to the park or the local shop.

Zara and Craig's mother agree that if Craig seems tired, he will have his sleep a little earlier in the afternoon, and that if he still seems very active at night time that they will get together to review how things are going in a few weeks' time.

Some points to consider

- *Was the right approach taken in this situation?*
- *What benefits was Zara trying to achieve?*

Developing strong relationships

Samantha is a 26-year-old who gave birth to her first child Connor yesterday. Samantha had planned to go home after a 48-hour hospital stay, but as the time gets closer she begins to feel unsure about her abilities to be able to look after Connor. She thought that understanding the needs of a baby would come naturally, but this is not how she is finding things. Even understanding why Connor is crying is difficult to interpret. Samantha has no family living close by and this is making her feel more vulnerable as a new parent.

The midwife speaks to Samantha about her plans for going home and asks how she is feeling about being a new mother. The midwife explains that often new mothers take time to learn this new role and develop relationships with their babies. Samantha, being given an opening to express her feelings, explains to the midwife how unsure she feels in her abilities to care for Connor. After discussion Samantha asks to stay an extra night in hospital. During this extra time in hospital the midwives take time to encourage and praise Samantha on her abilities to care for and love Connor.

On discharge the midwives plan to visit Samantha daily, to offer support and praise to help support Samantha in her skills as a new mother and her developing relationship with Connor. The midwives share this information with the health visitor to ensure that Samantha continues to receive the encouragement and support she needs: to help develop a strong bond and relationship with Connor.

Some points to consider

- *What do you think Samantha learned from this situation?*
- *After Samantha and Connor are home, what key elements of caring for Connor might the health visitor want to concentrate on?*

Important interactions

Linda is a single parent with a 2-year-old living in an isolated rural area. The nearest bus stop is one mile away and the service is very irregular. Getting to the nearest town by bus is difficult and during the cold, wet winter months Linda does not manage this at all.

The local Family First service offered her an opportunity to meet another adult one to one, who was to become Linda's volunteer. This now meant Linda could go for walks away from her immediate environment, have a coffee, go for a swim or just sit at home and have someone to chat to. Also on offer was weekly transport for Linda and her child to a Family First group, where her child could meet and interact with other children and where she could meet other parents.

Linda enjoys the company of the volunteer and has made new friends at the group. Recently, when the group was shut for a week, one of the other mothers from the group drove out to see Linda and they enjoyed a chat, whilst their two children played together.

Some points to consider

- *What are the benefits to both Linda and her child, of this type of support?*
- *Why was it important that Linda had choices to make?*

Time to reflect on your practice

Now, thinking about some of the bigger issues that arise from these examples, reflect on the strengths you have in your own practice and also some ideas for improvement.

- How can differences between parents' expectations and the setting in which children are cared for be sensitively resolved? What instances have you had recently? Are there strategies that might be helpful for reassuring your parents about their child's wellbeing?

- Which methods do you currently use to support and maintain key relationships with children and between staff? What evidence do you have that these methods are effective and that everyone feels included and that their needs are understood? What next steps do you see yourself taking?

- What are your key qualities helping you to establish the strong, reciprocal relationships with families that you need? How could you build on these?

- Why is it important for children to have ongoing relationships with their parents, even in difficult circumstances? Can you add anything further to what you currently do to enhance child/parent relationships?

- Does parenthood come as naturally as we often think it should? How are parents supported in your setting as they develop relationships with their new babies? Is there anything else that you can try?

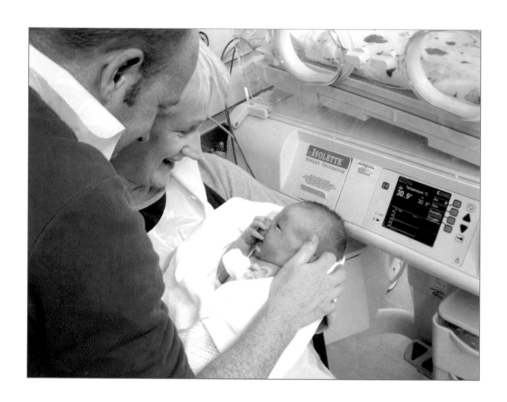

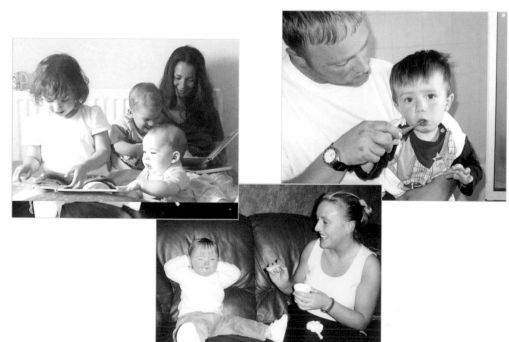

Section 4

Responsive care – promoting effective practice

Responsive care means knowing and accepting each child and respecting each child as an individual.

Establishing responsive care is one key feature in ensuring effective practice with young children and their families, together with good relationships and respectful approaches.

Key considerations for establishing responsive care include:

- building a knowledge of the individual child
- building an understanding of the needs and dispositions of each child
- ensuring interested, affectionate and appreciative adults
- using flexible, personalised and relaxed approaches
- working to enhance sensitivity and respect.

Responsive care is where the adult is highly observant of, and involved with, the child, demonstrating a sensitive approach to the child through words and facial expression, through touch and through physical closeness. Responsive adults are closely observant, are reflective and are in tune with what the child is trying to tell them, so that they can make sensitive decisions about what to do and how to respond.

Valuing routines

Children learn throughout their day, regardless and sometimes in spite of what adults may be doing or have planned.

Routines are an important part of the babies' and young child's day. They can also take up a large amount of time each day and this is why it is so important that routines are seen as valuable opportunities to be with children and to develop relationships. In an attempt to complete a routine task quickly, adults often lose a valuable opportunity to interact responsively with the child.

Respectful and well-informed physical care is really about handling a baby or young child with respect. It is not just a routine task. Respectful and well-informed physical care is crucial to establishing the relationships and responsive care practices talked about earlier.

Tuning into children effectively means recognising that some of the everyday activities and the more routine parts of the day, such as mealtimes, bath-times and changing a nappy, all provide valuable opportunities for adults to interact with children and for children to develop and learn.

Routines can offer many possibilities for the sorts of playful encounters that babies and young children enjoy, whether it is a game of 'peek-a-boo' during a nappy change, playing with a baby's fingers and toes, or taking the time to respond to children's humour while they talk over lunch.

Respectful and well-informed physical care includes:

- talking to, singing to and making eye contact with a baby whilst changing their nappy
- asking the child's permission to wipe their nose
- knowing how a baby likes to be held when being given a bottle
- noticing that not all young children like to wear plastic aprons to play in the water.

Where adults become too focused on adult-led activities and tasks, they may be in danger of forgetting about the individual child. Adults need to recognise that for the child, the process is often far more important than any end product and that allowing children to follow their own interests, at their own pace is part of respectful care.

Being sensitive, supportive and interested ensures that planning remains open-ended and flexible. It allows adults to make well-informed decisions about what resources and materials to provide and it allows adults to identify the value of what they have provided.

Opportunities to be with an adult who is affectionate, appreciative and relaxed are important to babies and young children. Taking the time to talk, smile, play with and respond to each child, to show them that they are important and interesting, can be done during routine activities. Many of the tasks that adults carry out during a busy day provide ideal opportunities for children to get involved. Unloading the washing machine, making a snack and wiping the table are activities that can become enjoyable if they are shared and children are allowed to become genuinely involved. Playful interactions during routines and simple turn-taking games also serve as a means of learning and bonding for babies and young children. Being aware of the value of routines can help to ensure that the child remains the focus and not the task.

It is also important to adapt routines to individual needs, interests, preferences and capabilities and this means ensuring that children:

- have opportunities to be involved or to opt out
- have the chance to have quiet times alone with an adult
- are allowed to be independent, practise new skills and do things for themselves, as well as have things done for them.

The most important thing about routines is to keep them as flexible and individualised as possible. Not taking the time may sometimes allow tasks to be completed more quickly, but misses out on the opportunity to be really involved with and connected to the child. Working with young babies who benefit from a sleep during the daytime does not mean that they all need to be settled and put down for their sleep at a particular time. Young children who might like a snack between breakfast and lunch do not all need to sit down together at the same time each day either. Having a flexible routine means that having a sleep is possible when you feel tired and that eating a snack is possible when you are hungry.

Babies and young children are very perceptive – they know when they are having things done to them rather than done with them. Being included in 'we' has great significance at any age.

Thoughtful and attentive interactions: are you tuned in?

Being 'tuned in' allows you to know the child. Adults who are important in children's lives need this knowledge to support children's development and learning. Being tuned in to the child means:

- being closely observant, attentive and responsive
- understanding what a baby or child's behaviour indicates
- interpreting the child's interests, thoughts and dispositions
- using knowledge and experience to help in making decisions
- being reflective and thoughtful about what you see.

In early years settings, a carefully thought-out, clearly defined and well-backed-up key person system should allow babies and young children to build the close, one-to-one, reciprocal relationships so crucially important to health, wellbeing and development. The key person system can promote significant relationships between adults and young children and allows the child to experience close, trusting and reliable contact with others.

Getting the balance right includes meeting the challenges of:

- staff turnover
- transition arrangements for children
- reaching a common understanding of what an effective key person system entails and how it should be backed up, so that the child always has someone available to them that understands and knows them
- ratios of adults to children.

Tuning in to children means that early years settings need to take account of these issues and their effects on quality.

Planning and flexibility, observation and reflection

Flexible planning, close observation and the ability to reflect on how things have gone all help adults to ensure that the environments children find themselves in are as responsive and thoughtful as possible.

Planning for young children does not mean organising every aspect of their day. Planning structures that remove the child's choice are not respectful of babies and young children. Planning needs to:

- be flexible and open ended, and allowed to be responsive to the changing pace and flow of the children's interests and enthusiasm
- be individualised and create familiarity for the child by making links with home surroundings
- be reflective, and allowed to be based on something that you may have just learned about a child, such as an interest in tractors, a fascination with patterns or a need for more quiet times
- be directed by the child's interests, needs, capabilities and preferences.

Babies and young children benefit from having access to different age groups. Babies like to observe older children as they interact and play. Older children learn important skills of looking after and caring for others by being given the opportunity to play alongside those younger than them.

Reflecting on how to organise environments effectively for babies' and young children's needs means adults need to focus on the value of talk, play, paying attention, interacting and spending meaningful time with children. Loose and flexible plans allow adults to choose the moment that is right for the child, to either introduce something new, or to step back and not invade the child's play.

Planning flexibly for young children also involves understanding the importance of continuity and familiarity to children and the importance of the day-to-day happenings in whatever setting they are in. Children like to return to and revisit things that were important to them that morning, the day before, or the previous week.

Adults who work with very young children need the time to share their observations of children, to talk, plan and to reflect, where possible, in groups. This not only helps to make sure that the provision for children is thoughtful and attentive; it also supports adults in a demanding and complex job.
If children are being cared for outside the home, they also like to revisit the key person they have moved on from and the room they may have been in as a baby or toddler.

It is important to value children's social life and what can be learned, on both sides, between, for example, a 3-year-old and an 11-month-old. Allowing children to have opportunities to be together, rather than being in a room with others simply because of their age is an ideal chance to promote the rights and responsibilities that the section on 'respect' goes on to talk about.

Planning for play

Opportunities for play that allow children to become deeply involved are very important. Babies and young children often benefit most from being able to concentrate on something in depth, rather than being surrounded by many different objects and choices.

Play is a very powerful tool that promotes children's development and learning. Play allows children to make important connections about what they know; it allows babies and young children to celebrate what they can do. Through their play babies and young children show observant adults how competent and skilled they are.

Adults who are sensitive and attentive can help to create play environments that encourage and support young children and that enhance children's play.

Being observant and reflective involves the tuning in talked about earlier; it involves acting upon what you have observed and what you have learned from tuning in.

When we plan for children and reflect on how best to support them, we need to remember the importance of the child's voice. The child's voice must not be neglected; the importance of it must not be underestimated.

Adults can effectively support children's play by knowing when to introduce a new object and when to interact as well as knowing when to step back and watch. Play opportunities need to:

- avoid unnecessary interruptions and restrictions
- recognise that children use everything in the environment around them for their play, not just manufactured toys
- reflect that children need to play with people as well as with objects
- recognise that play can include other or imagined people who are not present
- be accessible and adaptable to all children, in order that children's individual needs can be met
- be supported by adults who know how to extend and support children's play without taking over and spoiling it.

Adults need to understand what children's play is telling them about the child. Play helps children to find a voice.[4]

[4] Bruce, T, 'Play Matters' from Birth to 3 Matters Conference, 2003

Responsive care

Staff members decide to put out the water tray for the small group of children aged between 11 and 16 months, providing a range of containers for filling and pouring, plastic sheeting, a mop for any spillages and towels placed on the radiator to warm. The children get ready, and, wearing their nappies, begin to play with the water, watching it pour, splashing and dabbling in the water. Staff members sit around the children, watching them, smiling and encouraging the children through words and gestures.

Anna, 14 months, watches the other children. She has shown that she does not want to take part and has not changed out of her clothes. She edges closer and sits on Nicola's lap, who is her key person. Nicola talks softly to Anna, pointing out what the other children are doing. She takes Anna's hand and asks 'Would you like to feel the water Anna?' Anna nods her head and puts her hand in the water.

Anna then tugs at her top and shows Nicola that she is ready to get changed to play in the water. Nicola helps Anna to get changed and Anna sits for a while on Nicola's lap again, before reaching out towards the water tray.

Nicola sits at the side of Anna as she begins to play, talking to her about the water and showing excitement and pleasure in what Anna is doing.

Anna is splashed by the water as another child plays and she begins to cry. Nicola quickly takes Anna on to her lap, wrapping her in a towel, rocking Anna and reassuring her. Anna now wants to put her clothes back on. Nicola sees this and helps her to get dressed again, talking about each item of clothing as they put it on and giving Anna a cuddle.

Some points to consider

- *What do you think Anna learned from this situation?*
- *How did Nicola demonstrate that she was in tune with Anna and would you have responded differently?*

Feeling welcome

Sarah's baby, Iona, 5 months old, attends all-day care provision while her mother works at an office nearby. Iona is being breast-fed as well as taking solids and Sarah comes across to the centre each lunch time in order to see Iona and feed her.

Staff members have made Sarah feel very welcome by providing a choice of seating, a rocking chair and a low settee with comfortable cushions. When Sarah arrives she is greeted warmly by the staff and asked if she would like a drink of water or orange juice while she is feeding Iona. Both Iona and her mother clearly look forward to and enjoy having this cosy and satisfying time together.

Some points to consider

- *What are the key elements that staff members have recognised and acted upon here?*
- *Is there anything else that might have been done?*

Examples from practice

Robert, who is 3 years old, is a quiet child and seems to respond to the suggestions others make to him without appearing to have any particular wishes of his own. His childminder, Julie, is concerned that Robert is unwilling to make decisions and choices of his own, although this is now his third week with him.

Julie sets out a variety of activities for the children she cares for to choose from and encourages Robert to choose for himself. He begins by always picking the train set, so Julie plays with him, interacting with him and observing what Robert says and does. As they play, Robert begins to respond and join in more, talking enthusiastically about what he is doing. Julie uses this opportunity to ask Robert about what he likes best about what he is doing, and uses his responses to try and interest Robert in some of the other activities on offer.

Over the next few weeks Robert begins to make more choices for himself, which Julie encourages, showing interest and delight. Robert gradually appears more confident and becomes more interested in what the other children are involved in, joining in and making suggestions of his own.

Some points to consider

- *Julie took the time to observe Robert and reflect on what his behaviour was telling her. How might she share her observations with Robert's parents?*
- *What would you suggest she do to learn more about Robert from them?*

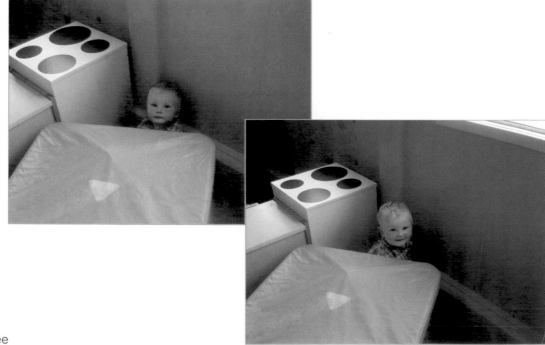

The right to explore

David, who is 3 years old, explores most comfortably by crawling around the play space at his nursery. He stops at a table with leaves on and pulls himself up to stand and examine the leaves. He moves on to the table with playdough and again pulls himself up to play with the dough. Occasionally he has a fall, but does not injure himself.

The early years worker observes him but does not intervene, encouraging him to continue his explorations.

Later on, when David has a snack, he reaches the sink to wash his hands using a step and sits with a group of other children where all the children choose and prepare their own snack.

Some points to consider

- *Why is it important that David has the same opportunities to explore as his peers?*
- *What other opportunities could be provided for all the children, to develop their skills of independence?*

Examples from practice

Observation and reflection

The 2–3-year-olds' room in the nursery is a busy, active environment catering for 25 children. The head of the nursery regularly spends time observing the children and the provision in each area of the nursery.

Recently, the nursery head has observed that some children in the 2–3-year-olds' room appear restless and unable to focus on anything, which the views of the staff confirm.

Together, the nursery head and staff review their plans and decide that they will plan for better use of both their outdoor area and their quiet room and agree to review at the end of each week whether individual needs are being met more effectively.

Some points to consider

- *Was the right approach taken in this situation?*
- *Is there anything else that staff might have done?*

Time to reflect on your practice

Now, thinking about some of the bigger issues that arise from these examples, reflect on the strengths you have in your own practice and also some ideas for improvement.

- What methods do you use to demonstrate to babies and young children that they are important and that you are keeping them in mind? Think about specific examples in the past couple of weeks. Is there more you might have done on these occasions? Share any concerns about any children in your care who may be missing out and need different strategies, perhaps because they are quieter.

- How do you use physical care routines to build on your relationship with babies and young children? How can you check that this is effective? Can you think of other daily occasions that might be turned into valuable opportunities to interact with children on a one-to-one basis?

- Thinking about encouraging independence and sustained play, what strategies have you found to be effective in encouraging children to make their own decisions and choices? Are there any more daily tasks and routines that could be used to extend these opportunities?

- Providing good, restful and welcoming facilities for breast-feeding mothers is an excellent way to build that early relationship with mothers and babies. What other mechanisms can early years settings put in place in order to encourage parents of very young babies or those new to a care setting to feel welcome and supported?

Section 5
Respect – promoting effective practice

Each child is an individual, a person who has the right to be responded to and treated with genuine respect at all times.

Establishing respect is one key feature in ensuring effective practice with young children and their families, together with good relationships, and care that is responsive to individual needs and circumstances.

Key considerations for establishing respect include:

- valuing diversity, in terms of children's language, ethnic background, faith and family circumstance
- respecting children's different experiences
- being sensitive to and understanding of differences, to ensure fairness, equality and opportunity.

All adults involved with children have an important role to play in ensuring that children's rights are actively promoted. Children's rights and the respect that they are entitled to must not be overlooked just because babies and young children cannot safeguard their own interests.

The importance of the rights of the child

The way in which we should respect children in Scotland is governed by legislation, most importantly, the Children (Scotland) Act 1995. The United Kingdom has also signed up to an international agreement, the United Nations Convention on the Rights of the Child.

The 'National Care Standards: early education and childcare up to the age of 16' are also founded on principles that reflect the rights of children and influence how services for children and young people are run. Importantly, they are based on the UN Convention on the Rights of the Child.

All of us, whether parents, carers, early years educators, health or social work professionals involved with children and families, need to fulfil the obligation to safeguard and promote children's rights.

Taking account of the diversity that children and their families have to offer enriches the experience for all children, as they learn about others and begin to appreciate and value differences and similarities.

At different times in every child's life, they will experience situations that make them vulnerable and in need of additional support and attention. For some children, the need for additional support will be more significant and sometimes long term.

birth to three **37**

Respecting children as individuals

Children's views and attitudes have begun to be shaped from a very early age. Being a member of a family and a community helps to determine individual children's attitudes and values. It helps to shape children as individuals and to establish their needs and preferences.

Children's needs and preferences are important. For adults who work with young children, respecting the parent's knowledge of their own child and learning from the parent about strategies for supporting and responding to the child are fundamental to effective practice.

Effective practice that recognises children as individuals can often be reflected in the level of understanding that adults have of each child. Adults who understand the needs and dispositions of children gain this important knowledge from:

- close observation
- a willingness to learn from the child and from those closest to the child
- flexible, individualised and inclusive approaches.

Children with additional support needs and children who are vulnerable in other ways also require the timely and individualised support and attention that feature in this guidance, as do their parents.

Respecting parents

Parents are the most significant people for babies and young children and they continue to be the most significant when their children spend time being cared for outside the home. The sensitive approaches illustrated earlier in this guidance help to ensure that each child continues to be viewed as a unique individual with their own ways of understanding the world, whether they are cared for in their own home, whether they are cared for outside the home or whether they are cared for within a group setting.

Often parents have a feeling that something has either changed or is not as it should be. It is important that parental views and concerns are listened to and that whenever a parent may think their baby or young child needs support they feel able to access further advice.

Most parents of young children seek support and advice about their children and both children and parents do best when help and support is readily accessible. This support can help to provide the resilience that children need.[5] Because all parents can experience feelings of isolation and the need for support, those who work with babies and young children are in a responsible position. Staff members who are closely observant and who have a sound understanding of child development are often ideally placed to offer the support and information that parents need.

[5] Kirk, R, 'Family Support: the Roles of Early Years Centre', in *Children and Society*, Vol. 17, No. 2, April 2003

Support and advice can be formal or informal. It can come from:

- early years practitioners, community health and social work professionals, who may find themselves in the position of being able to reassure parents who have concerns
- child health checks that may identify additional shorter- or longer-term support needs, as well as presenting early opportunities to pick up on vulnerable children and families
- relatives, friends and the local community who can offer important social and emotional support as well as practical help.

There may also be circumstances where staff members need to express concerns about the welfare of a child to other agencies. In situations where a child may be being abused, relationships with parents still need to be maintained, for the benefit of the child.

All those involved in work with children and their families have opportunities to offer support. Because of this, it is important to work collaboratively to ensure that important information is shared for the benefit of the child. Working in close partnership with others involved with the child helps to ensure that as full a picture as possible of the child is available.

Valuing respectful care – what does it look like in practice?

From a very early age, children are finding out about their rights, often through the ways in which others treat them. They are learning about expressing themselves, about their interdependence with others, about sharing, making choices and about their place in the world. Children are active citizens in the world and when adults make decisions that affect children they need to:

- think first about what is best for the child
- listen to children carefully
- take children's views into account.

Encouraging self-respect and respect for others can begin through the sorts of experiences children have. Children need to be seen as knowledgeable about themselves, with interests, needs and wishes that must be taken seriously. Young children need opportunities to:

- participate actively
- be involved in making choices and decisions
- be genuinely consulted with
- feel that their ideas and feelings matter
- see that their ideas and feelings make a difference.

Young children are also able to solve problems from a very early age and, if given the opportunity, can solve problems together. Encouraging consistent opportunities for children to make decisions and to participate in problem solving are important features in developing:

- self-esteem
- respect for others
- a safe and secure environment for everyone.

Safeguarding children's rights and ensuring that their interests, needs and wishes are taken seriously, is a responsibility for all adults; it is everyone's responsibility to make sure that children are all right. Where children are too young or are unable to express their needs and wishes through what they say, the supportive role of the adult becomes even more important, through sensitive interpretation of the child's wishes and needs.

Respecting babies and young children involves:

- taking children's concerns seriously, listening carefully to what children say
- and responding to children's concerns, however small they might seem
- valuing children's relationships, with their friends, their families, their pets and with the objects that are important to them
- giving children the freedom to express themselves, through group times and through cosy opportunities for individual attention
- helping children to understand what is and what is not acceptable, by responding to them positively, with encouragement and reflecting on what children's behaviour tells you
- showing respect through what you say and do and how you express yourself.

Children's feelings of self-respect continue to develop as they become more independent and able to do things for themselves, such as being able to wash their own hands and use the toilet, put their own socks and shoes on, serve their own food or pour their own drink.

All children need opportunities for independence and to do things for themselves. Where children's abilities to develop self-help skills are restricted, it is the adult's responsibility to ensure that the child is treated with respect and a deep understanding of the individual.

This includes:

- following advice from parents about their child's preferences
- planning activities carefully to enable all children to participate
- being observant and interpreting children's wishes sensitively.

As children themselves gain independence and the ability to care for themselves and others it is important that adults recognise that these opportunities continue to stem from a secure base – from being surrounded by loving, caring and secure relationships that can support them through transition and change.

Very young children have opinions and views. They benefit from opportunities to resolve situations through expressing their feelings and being listened to, both individually and in a group. They benefit from being included in decision making, for example about what to choose for a snack, about choosing and setting out resources, about how to solve a problem.

Children gain confidence when they can see that their interests and decisions inform what happens.

Experiencing transitions: supporting confident children

Young children may be cared for in the home by a parent, by grandparents or other relatives, by an au pair or a nanny. They may be cared for in their relatives' home, or by a childminder in the childminder's home. Many young children attend a parent and toddler group, a playgroup, a family centre, a private nursery or a local authority nursery. Many children may have multiple carers, spending some time at home, time with a childminder and time attending a playgroup or nursery. At times, children will also experience the involvement of others in their lives, such as doctors, health visitors or social workers.

Transitions occur as children move between settings, as they move in day care settings from one room or area to another.

Many young children are experiencing a wide range of transitions each and every day. Because of the many different experiences children may have in just one day, it becomes even more important that there is some continuity and similarity of approach in the ways in which the important adults in children's lives behave and interact, not only with the children themselves, but also with other adults that are involved with the child.

Having as full a picture of the child as possible is helpful when supporting children through changes in their lives, and this means that all those involved with the child need to work collectively and share important information.

Changes can be stressful at any stage in life, but for babies and young children they can be particularly challenging. Moving on to different surroundings, or having to adapt to losing a close friend as they leave a setting, make demands on young children as they learn to cope with a new situation. Parents also need support to cope with change and new situations. Because of this, the sensitive care and attention given to ensuring smooth transitions is extremely important and must not be overlooked.

When experiencing transitions, babies and young children need:

- experiences that reflect their own home life and culture
- experiences and routines that are familiar and welcoming
- familiar objects and surroundings that reflect the surroundings they are used to at home
- care practices that take them into account as individuals and that show them that they are important and cared about.

In day care settings, where children feel secure in the knowledge that they can revisit the familiar people and places that were important to them earlier, they will find it easier to settle into a new situation. This approach helps children, parents and staff to cope with change. Coherent and integrated services help to

Ensuring smooth transitions needs to involve, on an equal basis, the children, parents and carers and all the staff within the setting.

Relationships, respect and the need for responsive care matter when children are very young and they continue to matter as children develop and grow, and as they prepare for important events in their life such as starting school. In order for children to face change confidently and positively, they need the continued support of the adults around them.

secure the best start for all children. They can help children to cope with new situations and can ease transitions for children, parents and those who work with children and families.

Adults need to support babies and young children through change. They can do this by:

- working closely with all other adults who are involved with the child and making sure that effective and ongoing communication takes place
- providing warm and affectionate opportunities for talk and discussion, stories and play, which help children to express their feelings
- being closely observant of gestures and body language and asking themselves what the baby or young child is trying to tell them
- showing through physical contact that they are aware of the child's needs, through holding out their arms, through a hug, by picking the child up, and by providing a safe and secure lap for the child to sit on
- providing opportunities for children and also siblings to see one another and not be separated for entire sessions into different age groups
- setting aside the time to plan for and ensure smooth transitions
- deliberately building shared memories that can be revisited with individuals and in a group.

Throughout all times of transition and change in a child's life, it is important that the actions of adults reflect the three key features of effective practice:

- the central importance of relationships
- the need both to be treated and to treat others with respect
- the responsive and sensitive approaches that say to children that they are valued and important.

Supporting transitions

Four children in the nursery are due to move from the baby room to the 1–2-year-olds' room at the end of April. Staff members are aware that one of the children will be particularly difficult to settle and that one father is very uneasy about the move and about having to form a new relationship with another member of staff. He has been very happy about the amount of support he has received from staff in the baby room and is concerned that there will not be the same level of support once the move has taken place.

It has been arranged that there will be no new starts in the baby room until the end of May, freeing baby room staff to help in ensuring a smooth transition for the children.

Claire is key person to two of the children and is a familiar person to all of the children who are moving. She will move up with the children and will settle them with their new key person, which will help parents to settle to the new arrangements also.

When staff members feel that all is well and parents feel well supported, Claire will move back to the baby room and begin to prepare for the arrival of the new babies.

Some points to consider

- *How would you respond in this situation?*
- *How can the new key person begin to build effective relationships with parents?*

A community of children

Tracy is the childminder of four children, two who are at primary school, a 3-year-old and an 11-month-old baby. When the two older children return from school, Tracy encourages all the children to sit down together with a snack and share what they have done that day.

Everyone contributes to the conversation and Tracy includes the baby, by saying:

And what did you do today, Ryan? Shall we tell everyone? You played with the bricks, didn't you? And we went to the park. And then you had a lovely lunch – what did you have? Cheese toastie and … banana! Mmmm, you enjoyed your banana, didn't you?

Ryan joins in with gurgles and says na na.

Some points to consider

- *What are the benefits, to all of the children, of Tracy's approach?*
- *How might it serve as a useful reporting mechanism to parents?*

Learning together

Debbie and her 9-month-old son Ruaridh, attend their local parent and toddler group. Ruaridh has his first experience of being given a treasure basket[6] to explore. Debbie sits quietly alongside Ruaridh, ready to reassure him if necessary, as he explores the contents of the basket.

Ruaridh takes each item out and looks at it. He turns the objects over in his hands, shakes them and explores them by putting them into his mouth. Catriona, who is two and a half, sits next to Ruaridh, and begins to explore the basket too. She offers a piece of fur fabric from the basket to Ruaridh. Ruaridh hesitates but then takes the fabric from her, smiling when he feels it.

The playleader comes and sits next to Debbie and they have a chat about other objects that Ruaridh might want to explore.

Some points to consider

- *How do you think both Catriona and Ruaridh benefit?*
- *What other opportunities could be provided for Ruaridh and for Catriona?*

[6] A treasure basket contains collections of objects for babies to explore using all their senses. The contents are usually natural or made from natural materials which can be easily collected from around the house or setting.

Changes

Jack has just turned 3 years old and is due to start nursery school. His mother Pamela has just had her second baby Sophie two weeks ago. Pamela has recently noticed a change in Jack's behaviour, he has become very clingy and unwilling to do anything for himself. The health visitor had discussed the possibility of sibling rivalry and some of the behaviours Jack might elicit with Pamela prior to the birth of Sophie and therefore Pamela was expecting this might occur.

Pamela knew from her discussions with the health visitor that Jack would need more attention and love to ensure he did not feel replaced in his parents' affection by Sophie. Pamela included Jack in caring for Sophie and gave him lots of praise for being a good big brother. Pamela arranged times where just Jack and she would spend time together without Sophie.

Pamela also arranged for Jack's start at nursery to be delayed, so that he had time to get used to sharing his life and parents with Sophie and begin to develop a relationship with Sophie before he went to nursery.

Some points to consider

- *Try to list all the changes in Jack's day-to-day life, from his perspective.*
- *What other strategies might have been used to ease his stress?*

Building shared memories

Kirsty is 2 years old and in the process of being adopted. She has been in foster care for the last one-and-a-half years, due to her mother having an illness that prevented her from caring for Kirsty. Kirsty's mother is frequently an in-patient at hospital.

Kirsty's social workers have arranged a birthday party for Kirsty, just two weeks away from her adoption date and this will be Kirsty's mother's final contact with her child.

Social workers know this will be the last experience that Kirsty and her mother will share. Kirsty will need this memory, including video and photos from the birthday party. The birthday party also provides an ending for Kirsty's mother and gives her a place as Kirsty's mother.

The party is held in the foster carer's house. Kirsty's mother brings presents, but most important of all her presence at the party leaves important messages for Kirsty and allows images of her at the party with Kirsty to be kept.

Later, a meeting takes place a week before Kirsty's adoption, between her mother, social workers, Kirsty's adoptive parents and her foster carer. All of the information, including the presents, photos and video was shared with Kirsty's adoptive parents, as significant objects that were important to keep and that hold important memories for the future.

Some points to consider

- *Identify the difference in memories and the sense of personal identity for an 'average' 2-year-old and Kirsty, who has undergone many transitions from birth.*
- *How might Kirsty be helped in the transition to the next stage, of living with her adoptive parents?*

Time to reflect on your practice

Now, thinking about some of the bigger issues that arise from these examples, reflect on the strengths you have in your own practice and also some ideas for improvement.

- What strategies do you currently use to ease transitions for children and parents? What are the particular needs of the staff at these points? Take one instance from your recent experience – what would have been ideal from the child's point of view, and how far did you achieve it?

- How do you ensure that children's needs and wishes are taken seriously and how are children's decisions allowed to influence what happens? What single step might you take towards more inclusion of children in decisions?

- How do you plan for individual time with children? How often does this not work out? Try to analyse the weaknesses in your plans and how you might manage to fulfil them better.

- What strategies do you have in place for sharing information between staff members so that they have a good knowledge of all children, their families and their changing needs? How could you build on these? How might you raise parents' awareness of the way this works?

Section 6
Reflections

'My babies know I will look after them ... I'm their mum.' 'How do you look after them?' Mum asked, and Rosie said 'I make their teas and I tell them stories and I take them for walks and I talk to them and I tell them that I love them.'
Waddell, M, *Rosie's Babies*, 1990

Of course, adults always bring their own assumptions, ideas and feelings to their encounters with children. It matters very much how adults view the capabilities of the children in their care.
Gillespie Edwards A, *Relationships and Learning: Caring for children from birth to three*, National Children's Bureau, 2002

A child's pride in knowing and doing must be recognised and supported, too. Shame of not understanding, or of not being understood, is destructive of learning. The child who is proud to learn, and whose pride is recognised with admiration, will learn.
Trevarthen, C, 'Learning in Companionship' in *Education in the North: The Journal of Scottish Education*, New series, No. 10, 2002

The important thing about being looked after is that it is done by someone who keeps you in mind even when you are not there, someone who wants to know what you would like to eat, to play with, to take to bed when you go to sleep, who knows about how you began in life and how to deal with you when you behave badly.
Extract from Kraemer, S, 'Parenting Yesterday, Today and Tomorrow' in *A Professional Handbook for Enhancing Parenting*, Dwivedi, K, N, (ed.), 1997

We must have the courage to insist on the best, not just an adequate quality of education and care with 'fit persons' for babies and toddlers ... we need the vision to plan for whole human beings.
Selleck, D, and Griffin, S, *Quality for the Under Threes: Contemporary Issues in the Early Years*, 1996

Glossary

Key person system

A system in which each child has someone in the early years setting to whom they can relate, who has a special relationship with the child and the child's family and who is responsible for the child's care and wellbeing.

Genuine dialogue

In this context, a meaningful conversation between a child and an adult, characterised by close attention being given by the adult to what the child is saying.

Inclusive approaches

Inclusive approaches are those that clearly value and welcome the contribution of everybody and that take individual circumstances into account.

Reciprocal relationships

In this context, the relationships that adults have with children and their families, characterised by mutual interest, warmth and respect, and based on acceptance and an understanding that all feelings and points of view are important.

References and further reading

Abbott, L, Ackers, J, Barron, I, Johnson, M, Holmes, R, Langston, A, Powell, S, Bradbury, C, Goouch, K, David, T, Birth to Three Matters – *A Framework to Support Children in Their Earliest Years*, DfES, 2002 www.dfes.gov.uk

Abbott, L, and Moylett, H, *Working with Under Threes: Training and Professional Development*, OU Press, 1997

Abbott, L, and Moylett, H, *Working with the under threes: responding to children's needs*, OU Press, 1997

Adventures in Foodland: ideas for making food fun from an early age, Health Education Board for Scotland, 1999

Aronson, S, (ed.), *Healthy Young Children: a manual for programs*, National Association for the Education of Young Children, 2002

Bredecamp, S, *Developmentally Appropriate Practice in Early Childhood Programmes*, NAEYC, 1997 www.naeyc.org

Bruce, T, *Learning Through Play: babies, toddlers and the foundation years*, Hodder & Stoughton, 2001

Dowling, M, *Young Children's Personal, Social and Emotional Development*, Paul Chapman Publications, 2000

Elfer, P, Goldschmied, E, and Selleck, D, *Key Persons in the Nursery: Building Relationships for Quality Provision*, David Fulton Publishers, 2003

Gillespie-Edwards, A, *Relationships and Learning: caring for children from birth to three*, National Children's Bureau, 2002 www.ncb.org.uk

Goldschmied, E, and Jackson, S, *People Under Three: young children in day care*, Routledge, 1994

Gopnik, A, Meltzoff, A, and Kuhl, P, *The Scientist in the Crib: minds, brains and how children learn*, William Morrow & Co, 1999

Health for all Children in Scotland (Hall 4)
www.scotland.gov.uk/consultations/health

Kraemer, S, 'Parenting Yesterday, Today and Tomorrow' in *A Professional Handbook for Enhancing Parenting*, Dwivedi, K, N, (ed.), 1997
Lindon, J, *Helping babies and toddlers learn: a guide to good practice with under-threes*, The National Early Years Network, 2000

Murray, L, and Andrews, L, *The Social Baby: understanding babies' communication from birth*, CP Publishing, 2000

National Children's Bureau, *Everyday Stories: Working with children under three*, 2003, www.ncb.org.uk

Nutbrown, C, (ed.), *Children's Rights and Early Education*, Paul Chapman Publications, 1996

Parlakian, R, and Seibel, N, *Building Strong Foundations: Practical Guidance for Promoting the Social-Emotional Development of Infants and Toddlers*, ZERO TO THREE, 2002 www.zerotothree.org

Pugh, G, (ed.), *Contemporary Issues in the Early Years*, Paul Chapman Publications, 2001

Ready, Steady Baby! a guide to pregnancy, birth and early parenthood, Health Education Board for Scotland, 1999 www.hebs.scot.nhs.uk/readysteadybaby

Roberts, R, *Self-Esteem and Early Learning*, Paul Chapman Publications, 2002

Rodd, J, *Young Children's Close Relationships: Beyond Attachment*, Sage Publications, 1993

Selleck, D, and Griffin, S, *Quality for the Under Threes,* in Pugh, G (ed.) *Contemporary Issues in the Early Years*, 1996 www.surestart.gov.uk

SOEID, *A Curriculum Framework for children 3 to 5*, Scottish CCC, 1999 www.LTScotland.org.uk/earlyyears

The Child at the Centre: self evaluation in the early years, Scottish Executive, 2000 www.scotland.gov.uk

National Care Standards: early education and childcare up to the age of 16, Scottish Executive, 2001 www.scotland.gov.uk

Stephen, C, Dunlop, A, Trevarthen, C, *Meeting the Needs of Children from Birth to Three: Research Evidence and Implications for Out-of-Home Provision*, Insight 6, Scottish Executive, 2003 www.scotland.gov.uk

Trevarthen, C, 'Intrinsic motives for companionship in understanding: Their origin, development and significance for infant mental health' in *International Journal for Infant Mental Health*, 22 (1–2): 95–131, 2001

Trevarthen, C, 'Learning in Companionship' in *Education in the North: The Journal of Scottish Education*, New series, No. 10, 2002

Waddell, M, *Rosie's Babies*, Walker Books, 1992

Warden, C, *The Right to Be Me*, East Ayrshire Council, 2002 www.mindstretchers.co.uk

www.carecommission.com

www.healthscotland.com

54   birth to three